Leon Prado

The Art of Dream Control
A Beginner's Guide to Lucid Dreaming

Original Title: *The Art of Dream Control: A Beginner's Guide to Lucid Dreaming*
*Copyright © 2025, published by Luiz Antonio dos Santos ME.
This book is a non-fiction work that explores techniques and scientific concepts related to lucid dreaming. It provides a comprehensive guide for beginners, offering practical methods to achieve dream awareness, improve dream control, and explore the subconscious mind.

1st Edition
Production Team
Author: Leon Prado
Editor: Luiz Santos
Cover Design: Studios Booklas / *Ethan Reed*
Consultant: *Sophia Williams*
Researchers: *Daniel Carter, Maria Evans, James Mitchell*
Typesetting: *Oliver Hayes*

Publication & Identification
The Art of Dream Control: A Beginner's Guide to Lucid Dreaming
Booklas, 2025
Categories: Self-Development / Psychology / Dreams & Consciousness
DDC: *154.63* - **CDU:** *159.964.2*
All rights reserved to:
Luiz Antonio dos Santos ME / Booklas Publishing
No part of this book may be reproduced, stored in a retrieval system, or transmitted in any form—electronic, mechanical, photocopying, recording, or otherwise—without prior written permission from the copyright holder.

Summary

Systematic Index 5
Prologue 9
Chapter 1 Dream World 11
Chapter 2 Dream Reality 16
Chapter 3 Inspiring Stories 21
Chapter 4 Oneiric Science 26
Chapter 5 The Psychology of Dreams 31
Chapter 6 Dream Journal 36
Chapter 7 Reality Checks 40
Chapter 8 MILD Techniques 45
Chapter 9 CAT Technique 53
Chapter 10 WBTB Technique 57
Chapter 11 Reality Testing 61
Chapter 12 Dream Meditation 66
Chapter 13 Ideal Environment 71
Chapter 14 Dream Journal 76
Chapter 15 Adjusted Cycles 81
Chapter 16 Persistent Dreams 86
Chapter 17 Rapid Induction 91
Chapter 18 Conscious Awakening 96
Chapter 19 Astral Travel 101
Chapter 20 Dream Stabilization 106
Chapter 21 Controlling Emotions 111
Chapter 22 Oneiric Self-Therapy 116

Chapter 23 Exploring Scenarios 121
Chapter 24 Deep Journeys 126
Chapter 25 Dream Encounters 131
Chapter 26 Dream Training 136
Chapter 27 Creative Insights... 142
Chapter 28 Facing Nightmares 147
Chapter 29 Emotional Healing.. 152
Chapter 30 Shared Dreaming.. 158
Chapter 31 Self-Transcendence 164
Chapter 32 Dream Mastery 169
Chapter 33 Advanced Diaries 174
Chapter 34 Beyond Dreaming... 179
Epilogue 184

Systematic Index

Capítulo 1: Dream World - Explores the nature of dreams, discussing their subjective experiences and the potential for lucid dreaming.

Capítulo 2: Dream Reality - Discusses the characteristics of dreams and lucid dreams, highlighting the differences between them.

Capítulo 3: Inspiring Stories - Shares historical accounts of dreams that have influenced discoveries, art, and personal decisions.

Capítulo 4: Oneiric Science - Explores the scientific study of lucid dreams, including brain activity and therapeutic potential.

Capítulo 5: The Psychology of Dreams - Discusses the psychological aspects of dreams, focusing on the theories of Carl Jung and the role of the unconscious.

Capítulo 6: Dream Journal - Emphasizes the importance of keeping a dream journal to enhance dream recall and facilitate pattern recognition.

Capítulo 7: Reality Checks - Introduces the concept of reality checks as a method for distinguishing between wakefulness and dreaming.

Capítulo 8: MILD Techniques - Details the MILD (Mnemonic Induction of Lucid Dreams) technique and other methods for inducing lucid dreams.

Capítulo 9: CAT Technique - Explains the Cycle Adjustment Technique (CAT) for optimizing sleep cycles to enhance lucid dreaming.

Capítulo 10: WBTB Technique - Details the Wake-Back-to-Bed (WBTB) technique, which involves waking up briefly during the night to increase the likelihood of lucid dreams.

Capítulo 11: Reality Testing - Further explains the use of reality tests to question one's state of consciousness and induce lucidity.

Capítulo 12: Dream Meditation - Explores the use of meditation to enhance lucidity, control dream content, and stabilize the dream experience.

Capítulo 13: Ideal Environment - Discusses how the sleep environment and pre-sleep habits influence the quality of sleep and dream experiences.

Capítulo 14: Dream Journal - Provides advanced techniques for dream journaling, focusing on detailed recording and analysis.

Capítulo 15: Adjusted Cycles - Discusses the importance of understanding and adjusting sleep cycles to enhance lucid dreaming experiences.

Capítulo 16: Persistent Dreams - Explores the significance of recurring dreams and how they can be used as a gateway to lucid dreaming.

Capítulo 17: Rapid Induction - Focuses on techniques for quickly inducing lucid dreams, such as the Finger-Induced Lucid Dream (FILD) method.

Capítulo 18: Conscious Awakening - Provides strategies for maintaining lucidity once it has been achieved in a dream.

Capítulo 19: Astral Travel - Discusses the concept of astral projection and its relationship to lucid dreaming.

Capítulo 20: Dream Stabilization - Offers further techniques for stabilizing lucid dreams and preventing premature awakening.

Capítulo 21: Controlling Emotions - Provides strategies for managing and controlling emotions within lucid dreams.

Capítulo 22: Oneiric Self-Therapy - Details how lucid dreams can be used for emotional healing and self-therapy.

Capítulo 23: Exploring Scenarios - Focuses on the ability to create and manipulate dream environments.

Capítulo 24: Deep Journeys - Guides the reader on how to explore the subconscious mind through lucid dreaming.

Capítulo 25: Dream Encounters - Discusses interacting with dream characters as a means of self-discovery and conflict resolution.

Capítulo 26: Dream Training - Explores the use of lucid dreams for skill enhancement through mental rehearsal.

Capítulo 27: Creative Insights - Details how lucid dreams can be used to enhance creativity and problem-solving.

Capítulo 28: Facing Nightmares - Provides techniques for transforming nightmares into positive experiences through lucid dreaming.

Capítulo 29: Emotional Healing - Details the use of lucid dreams for addressing and healing emotional wounds.

Capítulo 30: Shared Dreaming - Explores the possibility of shared dreams and the theories surrounding this phenomenon.

Fontes e conteúdo relacionado

Capítulo 31: Self-Transcendence - Explores using lucid dreams for spiritual experiences and achieving a sense of unity and connection with the universe.

Capítulo 32: Dream Mastery - Discusses reaching a high level of control within lucid dreams, allowing for the manipulation of dream elements and exploration of consciousness.

Capítulo 33: Advanced Diaries - Details advanced techniques for dream journaling, focusing on detailed recording and analysis for deeper self-discovery.

Capítulo 34: Beyond Dreaming - Discusses integrating insights from lucid dreams into waking life for personal growth, emotional intelligence, and problem-solving.

Prologue

Few experiences in life are as intense, mysterious, and transformative as dreams. Every night, without fail, you cross the veil of reality and surrender to the dream world – a realm where the impossible becomes natural, where memories, emotions, and symbols intertwine in unique narratives. But what if, instead of being a mere passive spectator of these fleeting stories, you could take complete control?

Imagine yourself flying over mountains that defy the laws of physics, conversing with characters from your deepest imagination, revisiting moments from the past, or exploring possible futures. Think about the feeling of freedom when you realize you are dreaming – and that you can do anything. This is not a gift reserved for a select few, but rather a skill that can be developed by anyone willing to awaken within their own dreams. And that is exactly what this book will reveal to you.

Science has already proven that lucid dreams are real and accessible. They are not fleeting illusions or esoteric myths, but a phenomenon studied by neuroscientists and psychologists around the world. Great minds throughout history have already benefited from this power: inventors visualized solutions to their problems during lucid dreams, artists transformed dreamlike visions into immortal works, and wise individuals delved deeply into their own unconscious minds to find answers they would never have in a waking state.

But the central question remains: and you? Are you ready to access this hidden world?

Within these pages, you will discover tested and refined methods to induce lucidity in dreams. You will learn to recognize the signs that you are dreaming, to train your mind to question reality, and to use strategies that will make your dreams as vivid and coherent as the waking world. Furthermore, you will explore how this practice can expand your creativity, unlock hidden fears, strengthen your self-confidence, and even enhance real-world skills through dream rehearsals.

The awakening begins now. Do not let another night pass without discovering the power that has always been within your reach. After all, sleeping without dreaming is missing the opportunity to explore a limitless universe – a universe that eagerly awaits to be unveiled by you.

Are you ready to step through that door?

Then close your eyes, become aware... and awaken.

Luiz Santos Editor

Chapter 1
Dream World

Sleep is not merely a state of rest for the body, but a passage to a vast universe of subjective experiences, where the mind detaches from the constraints of the waking world and enters its own dimension, shaped by memories, desires, and profound symbolism. During this period, the brain not only recovers its energy but also reorganizes information, processes emotions, and, above all, gives rise to one of the most intriguing phenomena of human existence: dreams. These dreamlike manifestations, which can be both fragmented and ephemeral as well as vivid and full of detail, reflect the inner workings of the psyche and, throughout history, have given rise to interpretations ranging from divine messages to mere chemical reactions in the brain. Despite the numerous theories that attempt to explain their nature and purpose, dreams continue to be a fascinating and often unexplored territory that challenges the limits of what we understand about consciousness and the perception of reality.

In the universe of dreams, the mind breaks free from the constraints of conventional logic and the laws that govern the physical world, allowing for the creation of impossible scenarios, improbable encounters, and narratives that defy any linear coherence. In this state of suspension of the usual rules of reality, it is possible to experience situations that transcend everyday experiences, transporting the individual to contexts that can be absurd, fantastic, or deeply symbolic. On some occasions, the dreamer finds themselves completely immersed in these scenarios, without questioning their veracity, while on others, a sudden realization leads them to understand that everything they experience is nothing more than a mental construct – it is at this moment that the phenomenon of lucid dreaming arises. The experience of becoming conscious within one's own dream inaugurates a new form of interaction with this dream world, where the individual ceases to be a mere spectator and begins to play an active role in the construction and manipulation of their own inner reality.

This mastery over one's own dreams not only sparks scientific curiosity but also opens paths for personal discoveries and advancements in self-knowledge. Lucidity in dreams represents an opportunity to explore the recesses of the mind, confront fears and insecurities, stimulate creativity, and even enhance real-world skills through simulated practice. Since ancient times, philosophers, mystics, and scholars have sought to understand and develop techniques to achieve this state of consciousness within sleep, realizing that it could serve both for introspection and personal growth as well as for artistic creation and cognitive development. Thus, the world of dreams, often relegated to the role of a mere nighttime activity without major implications, reveals itself as a vast field of possibilities that awaits those willing to explore it with attention and intention.

Within the broad spectrum of the dream experience, there is a particularly intriguing phenomenon: the lucid dream. But, after all, what defines a lucid dream? In simple terms, it is one in which the dreamer is fully aware that they are dreaming. This awareness, which can vary in intensity from a vague recognition to crystal-clear clarity, completely transforms the dream experience. The lucid dreamer is no longer a mere passive spectator, but rather an active participant, capable of interacting with the dream environment and characters, modifying the narrative, and even defying the laws of physics that govern the waking world.

This ability to take control of one's own dream opens up a range of surprising possibilities. Lucid dreaming is not just a form of entertainment or a neurological curiosity, but rather a powerful tool for personal development, creativity, and the exploration of the unconscious. In the realm of self-knowledge, lucid dreaming allows the individual to delve deeper into their own inner world, confronting fears, resolving emotional conflicts, and accessing parts of the unconscious that normally remain inaccessible during wakefulness.

Imagine, for example, the possibility of overcoming a recurring fear, such as public speaking. In a lucid dream, you could rehearse speeches, interact with imaginary audiences, and experiment with different approaches, all in a safe and controlled environment where mistakes have no real consequences. Or, perhaps, confront a past trauma, reliving the situation from a new perspective, with the awareness that it is a dream and the ability to alter the outcome. The possibilities are endless, limited only by the dreamer's imagination.

Beyond the therapeutic and self-knowledge potential, lucid dreams also prove to be fertile ground for creativity. Artists, writers, musicians, and inventors often report finding inspiration in their dreams, using them as a laboratory of ideas where they can experiment freely, without the limitations of the physical world. The mind, freed from the constraints of logic and reason, can create unusual connections, generate surprising images, and conceive innovative solutions to complex problems. Many accounts tell of music that was composed, paintings that were painted, and inventions that were designed, first and foremost, in the dream world.

In the field of science, lucid dreams have opened new perspectives for the study of consciousness and brain function. Researchers use neuroimaging techniques, such as functional magnetic resonance imaging, to investigate brain activity during lucid dreams, seeking to understand the neural mechanisms that allow the emergence of consciousness within the dream. These studies can provide valuable insights into the nature of consciousness itself, one of the greatest mysteries of science. Furthermore, research on lucid dreams can contribute to the development of new therapeutic approaches for sleep disorders, such as recurring nightmares, and even for mental health issues, such as anxiety and depression.

Lucid dreaming, therefore, is not a trivial phenomenon or a mere pastime. It is an inherent ability in all human beings that can be cultivated and enhanced with specific techniques and practices. Throughout this book, you will discover the methods to induce lucidity in your dreams, learn to control the dream environment, interact with characters, and use this extraordinary tool to explore your own potential, overcome your limits, and transform your life.

The world of dreams is a vast and unexplored territory, full of mysteries and possibilities. Lucidity is the key that opens the doors to this universe, allowing you to become the protagonist of your own dream journey. The ability to dream consciously is an invitation to a limitless adventure, an opportunity to discover who you really are and what you are capable of. This journey begins now. Prepare to unravel the secrets of the dream world and discover the transformative power of lucid dreams.

Chapter 2
Dream Reality

Human experience isn't limited to the waking world; it extends into a subjective and fascinating dimension that emerges during sleep. This state, often treated as a simple mechanism for rest, actually harbors a complexity that goes beyond mere physical recovery. During sleep, the mind detaches itself from the limitations imposed by everyday reality and enters a universe where time, space, and natural laws can be radically different. This dreamlike environment, in which sensations, memories, and desires blend into improbable narratives, reveals profound aspects of the human psyche and has been an object of curiosity and study throughout history. Different cultures have interpreted dreams as divine messages, manifestations of the unconscious, or even parallel realities, highlighting the fascination and importance attributed to this phenomenon.

Within this vast world of dreams, the perception of reality is in constant transformation. Although most of the time dreams are experienced passively, without questioning their nature, there are moments when consciousness can emerge, allowing the dreamer to recognize that they are in a dream state. This recognition marks the fundamental difference between regular dreams and lucid dreams. In the former, events unfold without the dreamer's intervention, who is carried along by the narrative without awareness of their participation. In the latter, there is an awakening of consciousness that completely alters the dynamics of the dream, enabling questioning and, in many cases, control over the events. This awakening within the dream itself represents a transformative experience, opening doors to a level of exploration and interaction with the dream world that surpasses the limits of everyday imagination.

The transition between a regular dream and a lucid dream is not always immediate or clearly defined. Often, there are moments of hesitation, in which the mind perceives small inconsistencies in the dream narrative but hasn't yet fully established its illusory nature. These moments of doubt are essential for the development of dream lucidity, as they represent the first indications that the mind is beginning to question the presented reality. With practice, the dreamer can learn to identify such signs and use them as triggers to expand their perception within dreams. By understanding the dynamics between states of dream consciousness, it is possible not only to enhance the dreaming experience but also to use this ability for self-knowledge, creativity, and even personal development.

Common dreams are narratives that unfold in our minds during sleep, without us being aware that we are dreaming. In these dreams, we are like spectators of a film, carried along by a current of events that often defy the logic and coherence of the waking world. We can experience fantastic situations, encounter people who have passed away, fly through the skies, face imaginary dangers, or experience intense pleasures. All of this happens without us questioning the nature of the experience, without us asking ourselves if we are awake or dreaming.

The logic of common dreams is often distorted. The laws of physics can be suspended: we can fly without wings, pass through walls, breathe underwater. Time can behave in a non-linear way: the past, present, and future blend together, events repeat or unfold at different speeds. People and places can transform abruptly and unexpectedly. Emotions can be intense and volatile, rapidly shifting from joy to fear, from sadness to euphoria.

This lack of questioning, this acceptance of the dream experience as reality, even if absurd, is the main characteristic that defines a common dream. We are immersed in the narrative, experiencing it fully, without the ability to discern that it is a creation of our own mind. This absence of consciousness is what fundamentally differentiates a common dream from a lucid dream.

Lucid dreaming, in turn, is marked by the presence of consciousness. At some point during the dream, the dreamer "awakens" within the dream itself, realizing that what they are experiencing is not physical reality but rather a projection of their mind. This awakening of consciousness can vary in intensity. It can be a vague recognition, a feeling of strangeness, an intuition that something is not right. Or it can be an absolute clarity, an unwavering certainty that one is dreaming.

With consciousness comes the possibility of control. The lucid dreamer can, to a greater or lesser extent, influence the unfolding of the dream. They can modify the scenery, transform objects, interact with the characters, defy the laws of physics, and even alter the dream narrative itself. This capacity for control is one of the most fascinating aspects of lucid dreaming, as it allows the dreamer to explore their own inner world in an active and creative way. They become the director, the screenwriter, and the protagonist of their own dream movie.

It is important to note that the transition between a common dream and a lucid dream is not always abrupt and defined. Often, there are moments of "pre-lucidity," where the dreamer begins to question the nature of dream reality but is not yet sure if they are dreaming. These moments can be crucial for the development of lucidity, as they indicate that consciousness is beginning to emerge within the dream. Small signs, such as inconsistencies in the scenery or impossible events, can serve as triggers for lucidity.

Another significant difference between the two types of dreams lies in the sensory and emotional intensity. Although common dreams can be vivid and emotionally charged, lucid dreams tend to be even more intense. The perception of being dreaming, combined with the ability to control the dream environment, potentiates sensations and emotions. Colors may seem more vibrant, sounds clearer, touches more intense.

Emotions, such as joy, fear, ecstasy, or sadness, can be experienced with surprising force, often surpassing in intensity the experiences of waking life. This sensory and emotional intensity is one of the attractions of lucid dreaming, making it a unique and memorable experience.

In summary, common and lucid dreams share the same stage – the sleeping mind – but their characteristics and potentials are distinct. While the common dream leads us on an unconscious journey, the lucid dream invites us to consciously explore the vast and mysterious territory of our own mind. Recognizing these differences is the first step for those who wish to learn to induce and control their own lucid dreams.

Chapter 3
Inspiring Stories

Throughout history, dreams have played a crucial role in the lives of countless individuals, influencing discoveries, artistic inspirations, and decisions that have shaped entire civilizations. Since antiquity, accounts of revealing and premonitory dreams abound, suggesting that the human mind, when freed from the constraints of the waking world, can access a deeper level of creativity, intuition, and understanding. Historical figures, scientists, artists, and philosophers have frequently reported dream experiences that changed the course of their lives, demonstrating that dreams are not mere nocturnal illusions but rather portals to powerful and transformative insights. In many cultures, dreams were seen as divine messages or revelations from the unconscious, capable of guiding choices and revealing hidden truths. This universal fascination with the dream world persists to this day, fueled by extraordinary accounts of dreams that have altered the destiny of individuals and even entire societies.

Stories of inspiration stemming from dreams permeate all areas of human knowledge and creativity. Great scientific discoveries were conceived in the dream world, where the mind, unburdened by logical and rational limitations, managed to establish connections that seemed unattainable in the waking state. The solution to complex mathematical problems, the conception of molecular structures, and even technological advancements were born from dreamlike images and symbols that, at first glance, might seem abstract but contained essential keys to understanding real phenomena. This phenomenon suggests that dreams not only reflect an individual's concerns and thoughts but can also function as a mechanism for processing and organizing ideas, allowing creative and innovative solutions to emerge without the interference of linear thinking barriers.

Beyond science, the field of arts and literature is filled with examples of creations that originated in dream experiences. Many writers and artists claim that some of their most impactful works arose in dreams, where vivid images, complete plots, and even entire melodies were "revealed" to them. The mind, when exploring symbolic and unconscious territories, is capable of generating narratives and concepts that challenge the restrictions of everyday logic, paving the way for original and profound creations. This phenomenon reinforces the idea that dreams not only mirror the dreamer's inner reality but also act as an instrument of creative expression, providing new ways to see, interpret, and reinvent the world. Whether in science, philosophy, or art, dreams continue to be a fascinating mystery and an inexhaustible source of innovation, proving that the dream reality can contain answers and inspirations that transcend the boundaries of wakefulness.

One of the oldest and most emblematic accounts of dreams with historical impact is found in the Bible, in the Old Testament. Joseph, son of Jacob, possessed the gift of interpreting dreams. When he was sold as a slave to Egypt, his ability caught the attention of the Pharaoh, who was tormented by disturbing dreams. Joseph interpreted the Pharaoh's dreams – seven fat cows followed by seven lean cows, and seven full ears of grain followed by seven withered ears – as a prediction of seven years of abundance followed by seven years of drought and famine. Thanks to this interpretation, Egypt was able to prepare for the crisis by storing food during the years of plenty, and Joseph was elevated to a position of power and influence.

In Ancient Greece, dreams were considered a form of communication between gods and mortals. There were temples dedicated to Asclepius, the god of healing, where people practiced dream incubation, a ritual that consisted of sleeping in the temple in the hope of receiving a revealing dream that would bring healing for their illnesses or answers to their problems. The philosopher Aristotle, although he did not believe in the divine origin of dreams, dedicated an entire treatise to the subject ("On Dreams"), in which he investigated their nature and causes, demonstrating the interest of Greek philosophy in the dream phenomenon.

Moving forward in time, we find the account of the French philosopher and mathematician René Descartes, one of the pillars of modern thought. In his work "Discourse on Method," Descartes describes a series of intense dreams he had in a single night in 1619. In these dreams, he found himself amidst storms, strong winds, and phantoms. Descartes interpreted these dreams as a divine calling to seek truth and knowledge through reason. These dreams are said to have been a turning point in his life, leading him to develop the rationalist philosophical method for which he became famous.

In the 19th century, the history of science records a remarkable case of dream inspiration. The German chemist Friedrich August Kekulé von Stradonitz struggled to unravel the molecular structure of benzene, a fundamental organic compound. In 1865, after years of fruitless research, Kekulé had a dream in which he saw a snake biting its own tail, forming a ring. This dreamlike image inspired him to conceive the cyclic structure of benzene, a revolutionary discovery that paved the way for the development of modern organic chemistry.

Another inspiring example comes from the field of technology. Elias Howe, an American inventor, spent years trying to create an efficient sewing machine. He faced difficulties in designing the needle mechanism. In a dream, Howe saw himself surrounded by warriors carrying spears with a hole at the tip. Upon waking, he realized that the solution to his problem was to pass the thread through the tip of the needle, and not through the base, as was traditionally done. This idea, inspired by the dream, allowed Howe to finalize his invention, which revolutionized the textile industry.

In the field of arts, the Scottish writer Robert Louis Stevenson, author of the classic "Strange Case of Dr Jekyll and Mr Hyde," reported that the central idea of the story came from a nightmare. Stevenson dreamed of the transformation of a man into a monstrous being, representing the duality between good and evil in human nature. Upon waking, he feverishly wrote the basic plot of the novel, which became a worldwide success and a reference in literature about the dark side of the human psyche.

These are just a few examples of how dreams, throughout history, have been a source of inspiration, revelation, and transformation. Whether as divine messages, scientific insights, or artistic inspirations, dream experiences continue to intrigue and challenge human understanding, demonstrating that the world of dreams is a fertile territory to be explored and valued.

Chapter 4
Oneiric Science

The scientific understanding of lucid dreams represents one of the most intriguing advancements in the study of the human mind, uniting neuroscience, psychology, and technology to explore a phenomenon that, for centuries, remained shrouded in mystery. Initially viewed with skepticism, lucid dreams were long considered mere fantasies without empirical basis. However, as science progressed, it became evident that lucidity in dreams not only exists but can be measured, analyzed, and even induced through specific techniques. The investigation of this peculiar state of consciousness has allowed us to glimpse new perspectives on brain functioning, challenging the traditional understanding that sleep and wakefulness are completely distinct and incompatible states. The study of lucid dreams, therefore, not only expands our knowledge about the mechanisms of sleep but also raises profound questions about the very nature of consciousness and its possibilities within the dream state.

Technological advancements have played an essential role in the scientific validation of lucid dreams, allowing for the direct observation of brain activity during sleep. The development of neuroimaging techniques, such as functional magnetic resonance imaging (fMRI) and electroencephalography (EEG), has made it possible to identify specific activation patterns in the brains of lucid dreamers. Research has revealed that the dorsolateral prefrontal cortex, the region responsible for critical thinking and self-reflection, shows significantly greater activity during lucid dreams compared to ordinary dreams. This discovery suggests that, contrary to what was believed, it is possible to manifest a high level of self-awareness and logical reasoning even while immersed in the dream state. This finding not only confirms the existence of lucid dreams but also suggests that the mind can operate in a surprisingly sophisticated manner during sleep, challenging conventional notions about the limits of human cognition.

Beyond its scientific value, lucid dreaming has sparked interest due to its therapeutic and psychological potential. Studies indicate that the practice of inducing dream lucidity can be beneficial for the treatment of recurring nightmares, anxiety, and post-traumatic stress disorder, allowing the dreamer to take control of the dream narrative and reframe negative experiences. Furthermore, there is evidence that lucid dreams can be a valuable tool for the development of creativity, problem-solving, and the enhancement of cognitive skills. The impact of these dreams on mental health and emotional well-being continues to be explored, but the findings so far suggest that mastering dream lucidity can open doors to new forms of self-knowledge and personal growth. As science advances, lucid dreams are ceasing to be just a curious phenomenon and becoming a powerful tool capable of transforming our relationship with the mind and expanding the horizons of human consciousness.

Initially, the idea that a person could be conscious during REM (Rapid Eye Movement) sleep, the stage of sleep in which the most vivid dreams occur, was met with skepticism by the scientific community. Many researchers considered consciousness and sleep to be mutually exclusive states. However, starting in the 1970s, the pioneering experiments of psychophysiologist Stephen LaBerge at Stanford University began to change this view.

LaBerge developed an ingenious technique to prove the existence of lucid dreams. He instructed volunteers to perform predetermined eye movements (for example, looking left and right repeatedly) as soon as they realized they were dreaming. These eye movements, which can be detected by electrodes placed around the eyes (electrooculography), would serve as a signal to the researchers, indicating that the volunteer was conscious within the dream.

The results of these experiments were surprising. LaBerge was able to record the predetermined eye signals, demonstrating that the volunteers were capable of maintaining consciousness during REM sleep and of communicating with the external world, even while in a dream state. These pioneering studies paved the way for a new area of research: the science of lucid dreams.

Since then, several studies have been conducted to investigate the brain mechanisms involved in lucid dreams. Neuroimaging techniques, such as functional magnetic resonance imaging (fMRI) and electroencephalography (EEG), allow for the observation of brain activity in real time, identifying the areas that are most active during lucid dreams compared to ordinary dreams.

The results of this research indicate that lucid dreams are associated with an increase in activity in specific areas of the brain, mainly in the dorsolateral prefrontal cortex. This region of the brain is responsible for higher cognitive functions, such as consciousness, critical thinking, decision-making, and working memory. The increase in activity in this area during lucid dreams suggests that these cognitive functions, which are normally suppressed during REM sleep, are reactivated during the lucid experience.

Other studies have investigated the differences in the electrical activity of the brain between lucid and non-lucid dreams. Electroencephalography (EEG) measures brain waves, which are patterns of electrical activity generated by neurons. Researchers have discovered that lucid dreams are associated with an increase in the frequency of gamma waves, which are high-frequency brain waves associated with consciousness, attention, and the integration of information.

In addition to studies on brain activity, scientific research is also dedicated to investigating the psychological characteristics of lucid dreamers and the effects of lucid dreams on well-being and mental health. Studies indicate that people who have lucid dreams frequently tend to exhibit a greater capacity for insight, creativity, and problem-solving. Furthermore, the practice of lucid dreaming has been associated with a reduction in the symptoms of anxiety, depression, and post-traumatic stress disorder.

The science of lucid dreams is still in its early stages, but recent advances have demonstrated that this phenomenon is real, measurable, and amenable to rigorous scientific investigation. Research in this area not only expands our understanding of the nature of consciousness and sleep but also opens new perspectives for the development of therapeutic interventions and for the exploration of the potential of the human mind. The scientific study of lucid dreams represents a bridge between the subjectivity of the dream experience and the objectivity of science, revealing a fascinating and promising field for the exploration of the brain and the mind.

Chapter 5
The Psychology of Dreams

The psychology of dreams reveals that the oneiric universe is not limited to mere random images generated by the brain during sleep, but represents a symbolic territory where profound aspects of the psyche manifest. Since ancient times, dreams have been considered messages from the unconscious, laden with hidden meanings that can influence waking life. Within this perspective, Swiss psychologist Carl Jung brought a revolutionary approach by suggesting that dreams are legitimate expressions of the psyche, offering valuable clues about internal conflicts, repressed desires, and the process of individuation. For Jung, the unconscious was not just a repository of repressed content, as proposed by Freud, but a living and structured dimension, composed of the personal unconscious and the collective unconscious. Lucid dreams, by allowing the individual to consciously explore this inner territory, offer a unique tool for self-knowledge and psychological transformation.

The collective unconscious, according to Jung, houses the archetypes, universal patterns of behavior and symbols shared by all humanity. In dreams, these archetypes emerge through characters, settings, and narratives that express fundamental aspects of the human psyche. In a common dream, these elements manifest symbolically, often defying logic and requiring interpretation to be understood. In lucid dreams, however, the dreamer has the opportunity to interact actively with this content, asking questions, modifying the narrative, or directly confronting archetypal figures. This opens a field of possibilities for understanding one's own psyche and for the process of integrating unknown or neglected parts of the personality. The Shadow, for example, which represents the repressed or rejected aspects of the self, may appear in dreams in the form of frightening figures or uncomfortable situations. In the lucid state, instead of fleeing or being overcome by fear, the dreamer can face these figures, understanding their message and promoting the acceptance and integration of these aspects.

Beyond the Shadow, other archetypes can emerge in lucid dreams, such as the Anima and the Animus, representations of the feminine and masculine principles in the psyche, respectively, and the Old Wise Man or the Great Mother, which symbolize guidance and intuitive knowledge. Conscious interaction with these dream figures can provide profound revelations about the dreamer's identity and internal challenges. In this way, lucid dreams become a powerful tool not only for playful and exploratory experiences but also for deep psychological work. The dreamer can use this expanded awareness to resolve internal conflicts, strengthen neglected aspects of their personality, and tread the path of individuation – the process of becoming a more complete and integrated human being. Thus, the psychology of dreams demonstrates that, far from being mere nocturnal illusions, lucid dreams offer an extraordinary opportunity for psychological development and the expansion of consciousness.

The unconscious, according to Jung, is composed of two main layers: the personal unconscious and the collective unconscious. The personal unconscious contains repressed memories, forgotten experiences, unfulfilled desires, and unprocessed emotions that are specific to each individual. The collective unconscious, on the other hand, is a deeper and more universal layer, shared by all human beings, which contains the archetypes, patterns of behavior, and primordial images that are inherited from our ancestors.

Dreams, both common and lucid, are considered by Jung as a gateway to the unconscious. They function as a kind of "bridge" between consciousness and the unconscious, allowing repressed or unknown content to emerge to the surface. In common dreams, this content manifests symbolically and often disguised, requiring interpretation to be understood.

Lucid dreams, in turn, offer a unique opportunity for direct interaction with the unconscious. By becoming aware within the dream, the dreamer gains the ability to actively explore their inner world, dialogue with dream characters (which may represent aspects of the self), confront their fears and traumas, and access information and insights that are normally beyond the reach of waking consciousness.

Jung believed that the process of individuation, the development of personality towards wholeness and the integration of opposites, was the central goal of human life. Lucid dreams can play an important role in this process, allowing the individual to delve deeper into their own unconscious, recognize and integrate their shadow aspects (the "Shadow" in Jungian terminology), and develop a more conscious and balanced relationship with their own inner world.

The Shadow, one of the most important archetypes of the collective unconscious, represents those aspects of the personality that are rejected or repressed by consciousness because they are considered negative, inadequate, or undesirable. These aspects can include emotions such as anger, envy, fear, or personality traits such as selfishness, aggressiveness, or weakness. In dreams, the Shadow can manifest in the form of threatening characters, monsters, wild animals, or frightening situations.

In a lucid dream, the dreamer has the opportunity to directly confront their Shadow, dialogue with it, understand its origins and motivations, and integrate these rejected aspects into their conscious personality. This process of Shadow integration is fundamental for the development of individuation, as it allows the individual to become more complete, authentic, and balanced.

In addition to the Shadow, lucid dreams can also allow for encounters with other archetypes of the collective unconscious, such as the Anima (the feminine aspect of the masculine unconscious) and the Animus (the masculine aspect of the feminine unconscious), the Old Wise Man (inner wisdom), the Divine Child (the potential for renewal), and many others. Interaction with these archetypes can bring profound insights into the dreamer's psychic dynamics and aid in the process of self-knowledge and personal transformation.

The psychology of dreams, especially the Jungian approach, offers a rich and complex theoretical framework for understanding the importance of lucid dreams as a tool for exploring the unconscious and personal development. By becoming conscious within the dream, the dreamer gains access to a vast and mysterious inner world, where they can confront their fears, integrate their shadow aspects, dialogue with their archetypes, and tread the path of individuation, towards the totality of being.

Chapter 6
Dream Journal

In the process of developing consciousness within dreams, one of the most effective tools for expanding perception and strengthening the connection with the dream world is the dream journal. This systematic record of nocturnal experiences not only enhances the ability to remember dreams with greater clarity but also allows for a deep analysis of the symbols, patterns, and emotions that emerge during the dream state. The continuous practice of noting down dreams upon waking strengthens dream memory, training the mind to retain details that would otherwise be lost in the first moments after waking up. More than just a simple record, this journal transforms into a personal map of the unconscious, revealing valuable insights about the psyche and serving as an essential tool for achieving lucidity within dreams.

By establishing the habit of recording dreams daily, the mind becomes accustomed to valuing these experiences and differentiating them more clearly from the waking state. Over time, patterns begin to emerge, revealing recurring elements that can serve as triggers for the perception of the dream state during sleep itself. Specific characters, settings, emotions, and events tend to repeat, functioning as markers that indicate when one is dreaming. This systematic identification facilitates the training of the mind to question reality, making it possible to recognize a dream while it is happening. Furthermore, the journal enables a deeper dive into the symbolic interpretation of dreams, allowing each person to better understand their own fears, desires, and concerns reflected in the dream narratives.

Building an efficient dream journal requires discipline and a commitment to self-knowledge. The entries should be made as soon as the person wakes up, before dream memories dissipate. The accounts do not need to be extensive or perfectly organized; even fragments, keywords, or brief descriptions of the sensations experienced are sufficient to train the mind to remember more clearly. As this habit strengthens, the quality of memories improves, and immersion in the dream reality intensifies. This process not only favors the development of lucid dreams but also deepens the connection between the conscious mind and the symbolic universe of the unconscious, opening doors to a broader understanding of oneself.

The importance of the dream journal lies in several aspects. Firstly, it helps to strengthen dream memory. Most people forget a large part of their dreams within minutes of waking up. By acquiring the habit of noting down dreams immediately upon waking, even if they are just fragments or sensations, you train your brain to pay more attention to dream experiences and retain them in memory. Over time, the ability to recall dreams becomes sharper and more detailed.

In addition to strengthening memory, the dream journal allows you to identify patterns, recurring themes, and significant symbols that manifest in your dreams. By rereading the notes over time, you begin to notice that certain elements, characters, situations, or emotions appear frequently in your dreams. These patterns can reveal important aspects of your unconscious, concerns, desires, fears, or internal conflicts that deserve attention.

The dream journal is also an essential tool for the development of lucidity. By recording your dreams, you become more aware of your dream life, increasing the likelihood of recognizing that you are dreaming during the dream itself. Furthermore, the journal can be used to record the reality checks you perform during the day, the lucid dream induction techniques you practice, and the results you obtain.

But how to create and maintain an efficient dream journal? The first step is to choose a medium that is suitable for you. It can be a physical notebook, a digital file on your computer, or an application on your phone. The important thing is that it is something practical and accessible, which you can always have at hand when you wake up.

Upon waking, immediately write down everything you remember about the dream, even if it's just fragments, loose images, sensations, or emotions. Don't worry about grammar, spelling, or coherence. The goal is to capture the essence of the dream before it fades from memory. Use keywords, short phrases, drawings, or any other resource that helps you recall the dream later.

In addition to the content of the dream itself, also note the date, the time you woke up, the title you would give to the dream (if any), and any other detail that may be relevant, such as your emotional state before going to sleep, what you ate or drank, whether you used any lucid dream induction techniques, etc.

After writing down the dream, take some time to reread and reflect on it. Try to identify the most striking elements, the symbols, the predominant emotions, and the possible connections to your waking life. Ask yourself: What is the meaning of this dream for me? What does it reveal about my desires, fears, concerns, or internal conflicts?

Over time, the dream journal will become a map of your inner world, a record of your personal evolution, and a guide for the exploration of your unconscious. By cultivating the habit of noting and analyzing your dreams, you will be investing in your self-knowledge, developing your ability to have lucid dreams, and opening a direct communication channel with your own mind. The dream journal is more than just a record; it is a continuous dialogue with the deepest and most mysterious part of you.

Chapter 7
Reality Checks

The achievement of lucidity in dreams requires constant training of the mind to differentiate wakefulness from the dream state, and reality checks are one of the most effective strategies for this purpose. These checks act as anchors that reinforce conscious perception throughout the day and, with continuous practice, end up being reproduced within dreams as well. When this happens, there is a significant chance that the dreamer will notice the inconsistency of the environment and become lucid. The secret to the effectiveness of these tests lies not only in mechanical repetition but in a genuine commitment to the experience. Questioning one's own reality with mindfulness and true curiosity is what increases the likelihood of recognizing a dream while it is happening.

The nature of dreams allows absurd events to be interpreted as normal because, in this state, the mind does not apply the same rigid rules that govern wakefulness. A well-executed reality check should, therefore, explore these flaws in the logic of dreams, creating situations where the difference between the two states becomes evident. When checking a clock, for example, the time is expected to remain stable in the waking world, but in dreams, the numbers often change erratically. Similarly, trying to push a finger through the palm of your hand can be a revealing test, as this is impossible in the physical world, while in dreams, the body can behave unexpectedly. The choice of tests should be based on the ease of execution and the ability to insert them naturally into the daily routine, ensuring that they become an unconscious habit that will also manifest in dreams.

To maximize the effectiveness of reality checks, it is essential to combine them with critical observation of the environment and reflection on one's own experiences. Simply performing the tests automatically is not enough; one must be truly present in the moment and seriously consider the possibility of dreaming. Furthermore, the reinforcement of the habit can be enhanced with the use of a dream journal, which helps to identify patterns and recurring elements that can serve as triggers for lucidity. The more integrated this practice is into daily life, the greater the likelihood that the mind will spontaneously reproduce it during the dream state, opening the doors to greater control and exploration of one's own dreams.

The logic behind reality checks is that, in the dream world, the laws of physics and logic are often distorted or non-existent. Therefore, a test that works in a certain way in the waking world may have a different or unexpected result in a dream. By noticing this difference, you can conclude that you are dreaming and thus become lucid.

There are several reality checks that can be used, and the effectiveness of each can vary from person to person. The important thing is to choose a few that are easy to remember and perform, and that fit into your routine. Here are some of the most common and effective reality checks:

Check the time: Look at a digital or analog clock, note the time, look away for a few seconds, and look again. In the waking world, the time will have changed consistently. In a dream, the numbers may change randomly, become blurry, or display strange characters.

Read some text: Choose a short text, such as a sentence in a book, a sign, or a plaque. Read the text, look away for a few seconds, and read it again. In the waking world, the text will remain the same. In a dream, the letters may change, the words may become jumbled, or the text may transform into something completely different.

Look at your hands: Observe your hands carefully, examine the details, the lines, the nails. In the waking world, your hands will have a normal and consistent appearance. In a dream, they may look strange, have more or fewer fingers than usual, change shape, or exhibit other anomalies.

Try to breathe with your nose plugged: Plug your nose with your fingers and try to breathe. In the waking world, this will be impossible. In a dream, you may be able to breathe normally, even with your nose plugged, which indicates that you are dreaming.

Jump and try to fly: Take a small jump and try to float or fly. In the waking world, you will fall back to the ground. In a dream, you may be able to float, fly, or defy gravity in other ways.

Look in a mirror: Observe your reflection in a mirror. In the waking world, your reflection will be normal and consistent. In a dream, your reflection may be distorted, different from usual, or even show another person or creature.

Ask yourself "Am I dreaming?": Ask yourself this question several times a day, with genuine intention. In the waking world, the answer will be obvious. In a dream, the question can trigger lucidity, especially if you already have the habit of performing reality checks.

Push your finger through your palm: Press one of your fingers firmly into the palm of your other hand; in the waking world, nothing will happen. In a dream, it is possible for your finger to pass through your hand.

When performing reality checks, it is essential that you do not do them automatically or mechanically. You need to have a genuine intention to verify whether you are awake or dreaming. Question reality, observe the details around you, be present in the moment.

The frequency with which you perform reality checks is also important. Ideally, you should do them several times a day, at different times and in different situations. The more you practice, the greater the likelihood that you will remember to do them during a dream.

In addition to performing reality checks, it is helpful to combine them with the practice of mindfulness and with regular reading of your dream journal. Mindfulness helps to increase your awareness of the present moment, which makes it easier to perceive signs that you are dreaming. Reading your dream journal, in turn, reinforces your dream memory and helps to identify patterns and recurring themes in your dreams, which can also increase the likelihood of having lucid dreams.

Reality checks are a simple but powerful tool for those who wish to develop the ability to have lucid dreams. By incorporating them into your daily routine, you will be training your mind to question reality and recognize the signs that you are dreaming, paving the way for conscious exploration of the dream world.

Chapter 8
MILD Techniques

Having established a solid foundation with the practice of dream journaling and reality checks, it's time to delve into specific techniques for inducing lucid dreams. Several methods exist, each with its own particularities and levels of difficulty, but all share the common goal of increasing the probability of becoming conscious within a dream.

Intention Technique (Simplified MILD):

The MILD (Mnemonic Induction of Lucid Dreams) technique, developed by Stephen LaBerge, is one of the most popular and effective. Although the complete version involves more elaborate steps, the essence of the technique lies in intention.

Step 1: Before going to sleep, mentally repeat a phrase that expresses your intention to have a lucid dream. For example: "Tonight, I will remember that I am dreaming" or "I will have a lucid dream tonight." Repeat the phrase several times with conviction and focus.

Step 2: Visualize yourself becoming lucid in a dream. Imagine yourself performing a reality check and realizing that you are dreaming. Imagine the feeling of freedom and control you will have when you become lucid.

Step 3: Upon waking from a dream (even if it wasn't lucid), try to recall as many details as possible and write them down in your dream journal. Then, repeat steps 1 and 2 before going back to sleep.

Anchoring Technique:

This technique involves choosing a "reality sign" or "anchor" that you will encounter frequently during the day. It could be an object, an action, a sound, or anything else that catches your attention.

Step 1: Choose your anchor. For example, you might choose to look at your hands, check the time, or hear the sound of a bird singing.

Step 2: Whenever you come across your anchor during the day, perform a reality check and ask yourself if you are dreaming. Do this with genuine intention, observing the details around you.

Step 3: Before going to sleep, visualize yourself encountering your anchor in a dream and becoming lucid.

Reflection Technique:

This technique is simple yet powerful. It consists of cultivating the habit of questioning reality throughout the day.

Step 1: Several times a day, stop for a moment and carefully observe the environment around you. Pay attention to the details: colors, shapes, sounds, smells, textures.

Step 2: Ask yourself: "Is this real? Am I dreaming?" Don't answer automatically. Observe the details, look for inconsistencies or signs that something is out of place.

Step 3: Perform a reality check to confirm whether you are awake or dreaming.

Self-Suggestion Technique:

Self-suggestion is a powerful tool for influencing the subconscious mind. Before going to sleep, repeat positive affirmations about your ability to have lucid dreams.

Step 1: Lie down comfortably in bed, relax your body and mind.

Step 2: Mentally repeat phrases such as: "I am capable of having lucid dreams," "I will have a lucid dream tonight," "I will remember my dreams," "I have control over my dreams."

Step 3: Repeat the phrases with conviction and visualize yourself having a lucid dream.

It is important to emphasize that consistency and persistence are fundamental to the success of these techniques. Don't be discouraged if you don't see immediate results. Regular practice, combined with maintaining a dream journal and performing reality checks, will significantly increase your chances of having lucid dreams. Experiment with the different techniques, discover which ones work best for you, and adapt them to your needs. The journey to mastering lucid dreams is a gradual but rewarding process.

The complete MILD technique is usually performed after waking up from a dream, during the night or in the morning, taking advantage of a period when the mind is more likely to return to REM sleep (and therefore, to dreaming). However, elements of the technique can be practiced before going to sleep as preparation.

Step-by-step of the complete MILD technique:

Wake Up and Recall: Upon waking from a dream (naturally or with the help of an alarm), try to recall as many details as possible. Write everything down in your dream journal: the plot, the characters, the emotions, the settings, the symbols, everything you can remember.

Identify Dream Signs: After writing down the dream, reread the account and try to identify the "dream signs," elements that indicate it was a dream and not reality. These signs can be impossible things (like flying or walking through walls), bizarre situations, people who have already died, places that don't exist, intense and disproportionate emotions, or anything else that is out of the ordinary.

Focus on Intention: Get out of bed and move your body for a few moments. This will help solidify your state of wakefulness. Sit or lie back down in your bed in a relaxed but attentive state. Begin to mentally repeat a phrase that expresses your intention to recognize that you are dreaming the next time you have a dream. For example: "The next time I'm dreaming, I will remember that I'm dreaming," "When I see a dream sign, I will realize I'm dreaming," "I will have a lucid dream tonight." Repeat the phrase several times with conviction and focus, internalizing the intention.

Visualization: While repeating the phrase, visualize yourself returning to the dream you just woke up from. Imagine yourself reliving the dream, but this time, when you encounter one of the dream signs you identified, you realize you are dreaming. Visualize yourself performing a reality check (like looking at your hands or trying to breathe with your nose plugged) and confirming that you are in a dream. Imagine the feeling of lucidity, the mental clarity, the freedom to be able to control the dream.

Repetition: Repeat steps 3 and 4 (intention and visualization) a few times until you feel that the intention is firmly ingrained in your mind. The goal is to program your mind to recognize dream signs and become lucid.

Go Back to Sleep: After completing the previous steps, go back to sleep with the intention of having a lucid dream. Keep your mind focused on the idea of becoming conscious within the dream.

The MILD technique is most effective when performed after a few hours of sleep, preferably during a natural awakening in the middle of the night or in the morning, when REM sleep periods are longer and more frequent. However, you can practice intention and visualization before going to sleep as a form of preparation.

It is important to reiterate that MILD, like any other lucid dream induction technique, requires practice and persistence. Don't be discouraged if you don't see immediate results. Continue practicing regularly, combining MILD with maintaining a dream journal and performing reality checks. Over time, your ability to have lucid dreams will increase significantly.

The WILD (Wake-Initiated Lucid Dream) method is an advanced and challenging technique that allows you to enter a lucid dream directly from the waking state without losing consciousness. Unlike techniques that rely on recognizing that you are dreaming (DILD - Dream-Initiated Lucid Dream), WILD involves maintaining consciousness while the body falls asleep and the mind transitions to the dream state.

This technique is considered more difficult than MILD or other basic techniques, as it requires a high degree of physical and mental relaxation, as well as good attention control. However, when mastered, WILD can provide extremely vivid and intense lucid experiences, as the dreamer enters the dream with full awareness from the beginning.

Step-by-step of the WILD method:

Preparation: WILD is generally most effective when performed after a few hours of sleep, during a natural awakening in the middle of the night or in the morning. It is important to be in a quiet, silent, and dark environment where you will not be interrupted. Lie down in a comfortable position, preferably on your back, with your arms along your body.

Deep Relaxation: Begin by deeply relaxing your body and mind. You can use progressive relaxation techniques, such as tensing and relaxing each muscle group in your body, starting with your toes and moving up to your head. Or you can practice diaphragmatic breathing, inhaling slowly and deeply through your nose, filling your abdomen with air, and exhaling slowly through your mouth. The goal is to reach a state of deep relaxation, similar to that which precedes sleep.

Focus on Attention: While relaxing your body, keep your mind alert and focused. Choose a focal point for your attention. It could be your breath, the sensations in your body, a mantra (a word or phrase repeated mentally), a mental image, or the sounds of the environment (if there is any soft and constant sound). The important thing is to keep your attention focused on this point without getting carried away by random thoughts or distractions.

Hypnagogic Images: As you relax and maintain focus, you will likely begin to experience what are called "hypnagogic images." These are images, sounds, sensations, or thoughts that arise in the mind during the transition between wakefulness and sleep. These images can be fragmented, random, bizarre, or surreal. Observe them passively, without getting involved or carried away by them. Remain an observer, aware that these images are a sign that you are approaching the dream state.

Transition to Sleep: Continue to focus on your anchor (breath, mantra, image, etc.) and observe the hypnagogic images. At some point, you may feel strange sensations such as tingling, vibrations, buzzing, a sensation of floating or falling. These sensations are normal and indicate that your body is falling asleep while your mind remains conscious. Don't be alarmed or try to control these sensations. Just observe them passively.

Entering the Dream: If you manage to maintain consciousness throughout this process, there will come a moment when the hypnagogic images become more vivid and coherent, and you will feel "pulled" into the dream. You may see yourself in a dreamlike setting, encounter characters, hear sounds, and feel sensations as if you were really there. At this point, you will be in a lucid dream, fully aware that you are dreaming.

Dream Stabilization: Upon entering the lucid dream, it is important to stabilize it to avoid waking up prematurely. Perform a reality check (such as looking at your hands or trying to breathe with your nose plugged) to confirm that you are dreaming. Then, engage your senses in the dream environment: observe the colors, the details, the sounds, the smells, the textures. Interact with the environment, touch objects, talk to characters. This will help deepen and prolong the lucid dream.

The WILD method requires practice and patience. It is common that in the first attempts, you will fall asleep without being able to maintain consciousness, or that you will wake up in the middle of the process. Don't be discouraged. Continue practicing regularly, and over time, you will develop the ability to enter lucid dreams directly from the waking state, enjoying incredibly vivid and controlled dream experiences.

Chapter 9
CAT Technique

The enhancement of lucidity in dreams involves not only conscious practice but also understanding and manipulating one's own sleep cycles. The Cycle Adjustment Technique (CAT) is precisely based on this principle, utilizing knowledge about the natural rhythms of sleep to maximize the chances of experiencing lucid dreams. Unlike direct induction methods like MILD or WILD, CAT works by structuring sleep and wake times, adjusting wake-ups to strategic moments when REM sleep – the phase associated with the most vivid dreams – is at its peak intensity. This approach favors the occurrence of lucidity more spontaneously, making the process more natural and less dependent on forced attempts at dream control.

The effectiveness of CAT lies in how it reorganizes the sleep routine, conditioning the brain to wake up at times conducive to dream recall and increased awareness within them. The central principle of the technique resides in the gradual adaptation of sleep schedules and the use of strategic interruptions to influence the transition between cycles. During the period of applying the technique, the body undergoes a progressive adjustment, developing greater sensitivity to the recognition of dream states. This refinement of perception during sleep results in a natural increase in the frequency of lucid dreams, without the need for abrupt interventions or methods that require significant cognitive effort before bed.

Incorporating CAT into your routine requires discipline and careful observation of your own sleep patterns. As each organism responds uniquely to changes in the circadian rhythm, it is essential for the practitioner to make personalized adjustments throughout the process, identifying the most effective times for waking up and the ideal periods of wakefulness before returning to sleep. Furthermore, CAT can be enhanced when combined with other techniques, such as the practice of mindfulness throughout the day, performing reality checks, and continuous recording in a dream journal. This set of strategies not only strengthens dream memory but also prepares the mind to recognize the subtle signs that indicate the transition between wakefulness and the dream world, creating an environment conducive to dream lucidity.

CAT is based on the fact that human sleep is composed of cycles of approximately 90 to 120 minutes, each passing through different stages, including REM (Rapid Eye Movement) sleep, which is the phase in which the most vivid dreams occur. REM sleep periods tend to become longer and more frequent as the night progresses. The CAT technique seeks to take advantage of these longer REM sleep periods, increasing the probability of waking up during one of them and, thus, having a better chance of remembering dreams and inducing lucidity.

Step-by-step of the CAT technique:

Determine Your Habitual Sleep Time: For one week, observe and record the time you normally go to sleep and the time you wake up naturally, without the aid of an alarm clock. Calculate the average hours of sleep per night. This will be your habitual sleep time.

Adjust Your Bedtime: Choose a day of the week (usually a day off, such as Saturday or Sunday) to apply the technique. On the night before this day, go to sleep 90 minutes earlier than your habitual time. For example, if you normally sleep at 11 pm and wake up at 7 am (8 hours of sleep), go to sleep at 9:30 pm.

Adjust Your Wake-up Time: Set your alarm to ring after your habitual sleep time, minus 90 minutes. Following the previous example, if your habitual sleep time is 8 hours, set your alarm for 6:30 am (8 hours - 90 minutes = 6:30 am). That is, if you usually wake up at 7:00 am, the alarm should ring at 5:30 am.

Stay Awake: Upon waking up with the alarm, get out of bed and stay awake for a period of 30 to 60 minutes. During this time, you can read about lucid dreams, practice meditation, write in your dream journal, or perform any other relaxing activity that does not involve bright screens (such as cell phones, computers, or televisions).

Go Back to Sleep: After the period of wakefulness, go back to sleep. It is during this period, after the adjustment of the sleep cycle, that you will be more likely to have lucid dreams, especially if you combine CAT with other techniques, such as MILD or WILD.

Repeat the Process: Repeat this process for a few consecutive days, or whenever you want to increase your chances of having lucid dreams.

The logic behind CAT is that by waking up 90 minutes before your habitual time, you will be interrupting a sleep cycle at a time when REM sleep is more likely. By staying awake for a short period and then going back to sleep, you increase the probability of going directly into a period of REM sleep, which favors the occurrence of lucid dreams.

It is important to note that CAT, like other techniques, requires practice and adaptation. Adjusting your sleep cycle may be a bit uncomfortable at first, but over time, your body will get used to it. Observe how your body reacts to the technique and adjust the times according to your needs. Some people may need a shorter or longer period of wakefulness, or a different time adjustment.

CAT is a complementary technique that can be used in conjunction with other lucid dream induction techniques, enhancing their effects. By optimizing your sleep cycle, you will be creating fertile ground for the conscious exploration of the dream world.

Chapter 10
WBTB Technique

The transition between wakefulness and sleep can be strategically used to increase the chances of experiencing lucid dreams, and the Wake-Back-to-Bed (WBTB) technique is one of the most effective in this regard. Based on an understanding of natural sleep cycles, WBTB takes advantage of the brain's tendency to enter REM sleep – the phase in which the most vivid dreams occur – more quickly after a brief period of wakefulness. This approach creates an ideal moment to apply other lucidity induction techniques, such as MILD or WILD, enhancing their effectiveness. More than just a simple sleep interruption, the technique requires careful planning and execution to ensure that the temporary awakening favors a return to sleep with greater awareness.

The success of WBTB is directly linked to the balance between sleep time, wakefulness, and relaxation. To apply it correctly, it's necessary to wake up at a strategic time during the night, generally after four to six hours of rest, a period when the REM cycle becomes longer. During wakefulness, which can vary from 20 to 60 minutes depending on individual adaptation, subtle activities such as reading about lucid dreams, reviewing the dream journal, and practicing reality checks help reinforce the intention to achieve lucidity upon falling back asleep. It's crucial to avoid excessive stimuli, such as exposure to blue light from screens or highly stimulating activities, to avoid compromising the return to sleep and maintain the mental state suitable for the technique to work effectively.

Upon returning to bed, the final phase of the technique involves maintaining focus on the intention to become lucid during the next dream. Complementary techniques, such as repeating affirmations or visualizing dream scenarios, help strengthen this goal. Consistent practice of WBTB not only increases the likelihood of achieving lucidity but also enhances the ability to remember and understand one's own dreams. Combined with other strategies, such as dream journaling and mindfulness throughout the day, the technique becomes a powerful tool for exploring the mind during sleep, allowing for an increasingly conscious and immersive experience in the dream world.

WBTB is based on the principle that periods of Rapid Eye Movement (REM) sleep, the sleep phase in which the most vivid dreams occur, become longer and more frequent as the night progresses. By waking up after a few hours of sleep, staying awake for a short period, and then going back to sleep, you significantly increase the probability of entering directly into a period of REM sleep and, consequently, of having a lucid dream.

Step-by-step guide to the WBTB technique:

Preparation: Before going to sleep, set an alarm to go off after approximately 4 to 6 hours of sleep. The ideal time can vary from person to person, but generally, waking up after 5 or 6 hours of sleep tends to be more effective, as it coincides with a period when REM sleep cycles are longer.

Waking Up: When you wake up with the alarm, get out of bed. It's important to leave the bed to ensure you are truly awake and don't fall back asleep immediately. Avoid bright lights and bright screens (cell phone, computer, television), as they can interfere with the production of melatonin, the sleep hormone, and make it difficult to fall back asleep.

Wakefulness Period: Stay awake for a period that can vary from 20 to 60 minutes. The ideal time varies from person to person and can be adjusted with practice. During this time, engage in relaxing activities related to lucid dreaming. Some suggestions include:

Reading about lucid dreams (books, articles, reports).

Writing in your dream journal, recalling previous dreams and identifying dream signs.

Practicing meditation or visualization, focusing on the intention to have a lucid dream.

Performing reality checks.

Planning what you would like to do in your next lucid dream.

Avoid stimulating activities such as watching television, playing video games, or using your cell phone, as they can make it difficult to fall back asleep and reduce the effectiveness of the technique.

Going Back to Sleep: After the wakefulness period, return to bed with the intention of having a lucid dream. Relax your body and mind, and practice your preferred induction technique (MILD, WILD, or another). WBTB significantly increases the effectiveness of these techniques, as you will be returning to sleep at a time when your brain is more prone to entering REM sleep.

Maintaining Intention: As you fall asleep, keep your focus on your intention to become lucid. Visualize yourself having a lucid dream, performing reality checks, and exploring the dream world with awareness.

WBTB is a simple but powerful technique that can be easily incorporated into your routine. However, it is important to take some precautions:

Don't overdo the wakefulness time: If you stay awake for too long, you may have difficulty falling back asleep and feel tired the next day.

Don't force yourself to stay awake: If you are very sleepy during the wakefulness period, it is better to go back to sleep earlier.

Adapt the technique to your needs: The amount of sleep before waking up and the wakefulness time can be adjusted according to your preferences and how your body reacts to the technique.

WBTB is an excellent tool for those who want to increase their chances of having lucid dreams. Combined with other induction techniques and the regular practice of dream journaling and reality checks, WBTB can open the doors to the conscious exploration of the fascinating world of dreams.

Chapter 11
Reality Testing

The human mind operates under predictable patterns in the waking state, but in the world of dreams, these patterns can become fragmented and inconsistent. The essential difference between wakefulness and the dream state lies in the logic underlying the perception of reality. In our daily lives, we rely on our memory and senses to validate our surroundings, without questioning the veracity of the environment. However, when dreaming, these elements can undergo subtle or extreme distortions, creating a scenario where the improbable becomes commonplace. In order to explore this difference and utilize it to achieve lucidity in dreams, reality tests emerge as a fundamental tool. They allow the practitioner to develop a continuous critical sense about their existence, breaking with the automatic acceptance of reality and encouraging constant investigation of the environment. Over time, this mental habit solidifies, allowing the same questioning attitude to manifest in dreams, where perceptual inconsistencies become evident and reveal the true nature of the dream state.

The process of performing reality tests is not just a mechanical act, but rather a practice that requires mindfulness and cognitive engagement. The mind needs to be trained to recognize patterns and look for anomalies that may indicate a dream. In the waking state, physical phenomena obey fixed and immutable rules: a light switch works consistently, reading text remains stable, and gravity acts uniformly. In dreams, however, these same rules become malleable, allowing objects to change shape, written phrases to alter when reread, and gravity to behave erratically. Thus, each reality test must be performed with genuine intention and a critical eye, avoiding automatisms that compromise its effectiveness. Only by incorporating genuine doubt into the act of questioning reality will the practitioner be able to carry this practice into their dreams, significantly increasing their chances of achieving lucidity.

Building an effective habit depends on the regularity and variety of reality tests. Incorporating them into routine moments, such as walking through a doorway, checking the time, or looking at your own hands, creates mental triggers that strengthen the practice. However, always repeating the same test can lead to unconscious adaptation, reducing its impact. Alternating between different methods, trying new approaches, and being attentive to moments when reality seems slightly incoherent help keep the mind alert. When this practice transfers to the dream world, the signs of inconsistency become clear, allowing the individual to perceive the true nature of the experience and take control of their own dream. Mastering this technique, combined with other strategies such as dream journaling and mindfulness practice, forms the basis for an increasingly deeper journey into the universe of lucid dreams.

The effectiveness of reality tests lies in the difference between how the waking world and the dream world function. While physical reality follows consistent and predictable laws, the reality of dreams is fluid, mutable, and often illogical. A test that works in a certain way in the waking state can have a completely different or unexpected result in a dream, revealing its illusory nature.

Correct Use of Reality Tests:

The key to the success of reality tests is not the quantity, but the quality with which they are performed. It is not enough to perform the actions mechanically; it is necessary to have a genuine intention to question reality, to be present in the moment, and to observe the results attentively.

When performing a reality test, follow these steps:

Intention: Before performing the test, pause for a moment and sincerely ask yourself: "Am I dreaming?". Do not answer automatically. Let the question echo in your mind.

Action: Perform the chosen reality test (see examples in Chapter 6). Do it with mindfulness, observing every detail of the process.

Observation: Carefully observe the result of the test. Does it correspond to what you would expect in the waking world? Or is there something strange, illogical, or impossible happening?

Conclusion: Based on the result of the test, conclude whether you are awake or dreaming. Even if the result indicates that you are awake, reinforce the intention to remember to perform reality tests in your dreams.

Ideal Frequency of Reality Tests:

There is no magic number of times you should perform reality tests per day. The important thing is that you do them regularly and at different times and situations. A good initial goal is to perform 5 to 10 reality tests per day, distributed throughout the day.

Some suggestions for moments to perform reality tests:

Upon waking up (even before getting out of bed).
Before and after meals.
When entering and leaving a room or building.
When meeting a friend or family member.
When encountering something unusual or unexpected.
When performing a routine action (such as washing your hands, opening a door, etc.).
When reading or watching something related to lucid dreams.
Whenever you remember.

Variation of Reality Tests:

It is recommended to vary the reality tests you use. If you always use the same test, you may end up automating the action and losing the genuine intention to question reality. Alternate between the different tests (see Chapter 6), choose the ones that work best for you, and add new tests to your practice.

Reality Tests and Lucid Dreams:

With consistent practice, reality tests will become a deeply ingrained habit in your mind. This habit will transfer to your dreams, and you will begin to perform the tests spontaneously during sleep. Upon noticing the inconsistency of the result in the dream world, you will have an insight: "I'm dreaming!". This is the moment of lucidity.

Remember that reality tests are just one tool. They do not guarantee lucidity, but they significantly increase the chances of achieving it. Combine the practice of reality tests with maintaining a dream journal, practicing induction techniques (MILD, WILD, WBTB), and cultivating mindfulness to achieve the best results.

Chapter 12
Dream Meditation

The human mind operates in a constant flux of thoughts, emotions, and sensory stimuli, creating a state of distraction that often obscures conscious perception. However, throughout history, various spiritual and philosophical traditions have discovered that meditation can act as a bridge between wakefulness and the dream world, allowing for an expanded state of awareness that transcends the barriers of ordinary perception. When applied to the practice of lucid dreaming, meditation not only facilitates the recognition of the dream experience but also strengthens the dreamer's stability and control within this fluid universe. Through the cultivation of mindfulness, emotional regulation, and memory enhancement, this ancient practice becomes a valuable tool for those seeking to deepen their exploration of the dream world.

By training the mind to remain present in the moment, meditation reduces mental scattering and promotes a sharper awareness of reality, a crucial element for the development of dream lucidity. The habit of observing thoughts without getting carried away by them naturally transfers to dreams, making it easier to recognize signs of inconsistency in the dream environment. Furthermore, meditation strengthens the ability to remain calm in the face of unexpected stimuli, reducing the likelihood of an abrupt awakening caused by excessive excitement upon realizing one is dreaming. This emotional stability also allows the dreamer to interact with the dream scenario in a more controlled manner, prolonging the experience and exploring its possibilities more consciously.

Another essential benefit of meditation in the practice of lucid dreaming lies in its influence on memory. By reducing mental turbulence and improving the ability to retain information, meditation aids in dream recall and the identification of recurring patterns, fundamental factors for those who wish to achieve lucidity more frequently. This improvement in memory, combined with the development of mindfulness, strengthens the connection between the waking state and the dream world, allowing the practitioner to establish a continuity between the two realities. By integrating meditation with other induction techniques, such as reality checks and dream journaling, it is possible to create a solid foundation for more lucid, stable, and enriching dream experiences.

Meditation, in its various forms, involves the training of attention and the development of full awareness of the present moment (mindfulness). This regular practice calms the mind, reduces the flow of random thoughts, and increases the capacity for concentration and focus. These benefits extend to the dream world, facilitating the recognition of lucidity and the control of the dream experience.

How Meditation Aids in Lucidity:

Increased Awareness: Meditation, especially the practice of mindfulness, cultivates the ability to observe one's own thoughts, emotions, and sensations without judgment or attachment. This heightened awareness transfers to the dream state, making it easier to perceive the signs that one is dreaming and, consequently, achieve lucidity.

Reduced Reactivity: Meditation helps reduce emotional reactivity, that is, the tendency to react automatically to internal or external stimuli. In the context of dreams, this means that the dreamer is less likely to be carried away by intense emotions or bizarre events, which could hinder the recognition of lucidity.

Improved Memory: Regular meditation practice has been associated with improvements in memory, both working memory (the ability to retain information for short periods) and long-term memory. A sharper memory facilitates dream recall, which is fundamental for the development of lucidity and for the analysis of dream patterns in a dream journal.

Greater Mental Clarity: Meditation promotes a state of mental clarity, reducing "brain fog" and the incessant flow of thoughts. This clarity facilitates the perception of details in the dream environment and the recognition of inconsistencies that may indicate one is dreaming.

How Meditation Aids in Dream Stability:

Attention Control: Meditation trains the ability to direct and sustain attention on a specific object (such as the breath, a mantra, or a mental image). This control of attention is crucial for maintaining lucidity in a dream, preventing the dreamer from being distracted by dream stimuli or from losing consciousness and returning to an ordinary dream.

Emotional Equanimity: Meditation cultivates equanimity, the ability to remain calm and serene in the face of intense emotions or challenging situations. In lucid dreams, equanimity helps to avoid excessive excitement, which can lead to premature awakening, and to deal with negative emotions, such as fear, which can destabilize the dream.

Presence in the Moment: The practice of mindfulness anchors awareness in the present moment, reducing the mind's tendency to wander or worry about the future. This presence in the moment is essential for maintaining lucidity in a dream, allowing the dreamer to fully enjoy the experience and explore the dream environment consciously.

Dream Meditation Practice:

There is no single "dream meditation." You can adapt traditional meditation techniques to the context of lucid dreaming. Here are some suggestions:

Mindfulness Meditation: Before going to sleep, practice mindfulness meditation, focusing on your breath, the sensations in your body, or the sounds in your environment. Visualize yourself becoming lucid in a dream.

Visualization Meditation: Visualize yourself in a lucid dream, performing reality checks, exploring the dream environment, and interacting with characters.

Mantra Meditation: Mentally repeat a mantra related to lucid dreaming, such as "I am dreaming" or "I am conscious."

Guided Meditation: Use guided meditation audio with a focus on lucid dreaming.

Meditation is a complementary practice to lucid dream induction techniques and reality checks. By cultivating awareness, attention, equanimity, and mental clarity, meditation strengthens the foundation for the conscious exploration of the dream world, making the dream journey richer, deeper, and more transformative.

Chapter 13
Ideal Environment

A good night's sleep isn't just about the duration; it's also about the conditions surrounding this essential state for mental and physical well-being. The environment where we sleep plays a crucial role in the depth of our rest and the vividness of our dream experiences. Creating a suitable space for sleep can directly influence our ability to achieve lucid dreams, as external factors like lighting, temperature, and noise affect the transitions between sleep stages and the duration of REM sleep, the period when dreams become most intense and clear. An optimized environment not only fosters the deep relaxation needed to reach lucidity but also minimizes disturbances that can fragment our sleep or hinder dream recall upon waking.

Beyond the physical aspects of the environment, our mental preparation before sleep also impacts the quality of our dream experiences. Visual and symbolic elements can act as triggers for our subconscious, reinforcing our intention to become lucid in our dreams. Having meaningful objects in the bedroom, such as an accessible dream journal, inspiring images, or symbols related to the dream world, can strengthen the connection between our waking reality and the dream experience. Practicing relaxation techniques before bed, like meditation or deep breathing exercises, helps induce a state of mental serenity, making it easier to consciously immerse ourselves in the world of dreams.

Another vital aspect of creating the ideal environment for lucid dreams is the consistency of our sleep habits. Establishing a regular routine, going to bed and waking up around the same time every day (even on weekends), helps regulate our body's natural sleep-wake cycle, maximizing the time we spend in REM sleep. Techniques like Wake-Back-to-Bed (WBTB) specifically target the periods when dreams are typically longer and more frequent, increasing the likelihood of lucidity. Adjusting our nighttime habits, such as avoiding blue light before sleep, reducing stressful stimuli, and having a light evening meal, can also optimize our transition into deep sleep and, consequently, into clearer and more controllable dream experiences. By aligning our external environment with proper mental preparation and a consistent routine, we create a fertile ground for exploring the full potential of lucid dreams.

Setting Up Your Environment:

Your bedroom is your sleep sanctuary, the gateway to the world of dreams. Therefore, it's essential that it's an environment that promotes relaxation, tranquility, and security – all crucial for inducing lucid dreams.

Darkness: Darkness is fundamental for the production of melatonin, the sleep hormone that regulates our sleep-wake cycle. Ensure your room is as dark as possible. Use blackout curtains, seal any light leaks, and cover or turn off electronic devices that emit light (like standby LEDs). If necessary, use a sleep mask.

Silence: Silence is equally important for restorative sleep and inducing lucid dreams. External noises can disrupt your sleep, make it harder to concentrate, and even prevent lucid dreams from occurring. If you live in a noisy area, consider using earplugs or a white noise machine (a consistent, monotonous sound that masks other noises).

Temperature: The ideal room temperature for sleep varies from person to person, but generally, a slightly cool environment (between 18°C and 22°C or 64°F and 72°F) is more conducive to sleep than a warm one. Adjust your room's temperature to your preference, but avoid extreme heat or cold.

Comfort: Comfort is essential for quality sleep. Invest in a mattress, pillows, and bedding that are comfortable and suit your needs. Make sure your room is clean, organized, and free of distractions.

Safety: Feeling secure in your sleep environment is crucial for relaxing and letting go into the world of dreams. Ensure your doors and windows are locked, and if it makes you feel safer, you can leave a dim night light on.

Dream Reminders: While darkness and silence are important, you can incorporate elements that remind you of your intention to dream. A dream catcher or another object that symbolizes this intention can be helpful.

Ideal Timing:

Your sleep schedule also plays a significant role in inducing lucid dreams. As mentioned earlier, REM sleep periods, when the most vivid dreams occur, tend to become longer and more frequent as the night progresses.

Regular Sleep Cycle: Maintaining a regular sleep cycle, going to bed and waking up at the same time every day (including weekends), helps regulate your body's biological clock and optimize your REM sleep cycles.

WBTB and CAT Techniques: The Wake-Back-to-Bed (WBTB) and Cycle Adjustment Technique (CAT) (detailed in previous chapters) specifically leverage the times when REM sleep periods are longer. By waking up after a few hours of sleep and then going back to sleep, you increase the likelihood of entering directly into a REM sleep period.

Naps: Short naps (20 to 30 minutes) during the day can increase your chances of having lucid dreams, especially if you practice the MILD (Mnemonic Induction of Lucid Dreams) technique before taking the nap.

Avoid Alcohol and Caffeine: Avoid consuming alcohol and caffeine before bed. These substances can interfere with your sleep quality, reduce the duration of your REM sleep periods, and make it harder to experience lucid dreams.

While there's no "magic time" to have lucid dreams, combining a sleep-conducive environment with optimized sleep timing, focusing on the longer REM sleep periods, can significantly increase your chances of success. Remember that everyone is different, and what works best for one person may not work for another. Experiment with different environment setups and sleep schedules, observe how your body reacts, and adapt the strategies to your individual needs.

Chapter 14
Dream Journal

The human mind processes a vast amount of information daily, and dreams are a manifestation of this immense flow of experiences, emotions, and thoughts. However, the fleeting nature of dreams often causes them to dissipate quickly upon waking, leaving behind only vague and disconnected fragments. For those seeking to better understand their own dream world and develop the ability to have lucid dreams, the practice of dream journaling becomes an essential tool. More than just a simple record, it functions as an instrument of self-knowledge, allowing for the identification of recurring patterns, significant symbols, and predominant emotions. Through writing, the dreamer strengthens their dream recall and establishes a bridge between the waking state and the dream universe, creating a continuous cycle of learning and exploration.

The effectiveness of a dream journal is directly related to how the entries are made. It is not enough to simply jot down a vague or generalized summary; it is crucial to capture sensory details, the emotions experienced, and any element that seems peculiar or striking. The richer and more detailed the description, the greater the ability to remember dreams and recognize patterns over time. Furthermore, the regular practice of writing stimulates the brain to give greater importance to dream experiences, increasing the frequency and vividness of remembered dreams. This structured approach allows the dreamer to become familiar with elements that frequently appear in their dreams, facilitating the recognition of so-called "dream signs" – clues that indicate one is dreaming and that can be used to achieve lucidity.

Another crucial aspect of the dream journal is its analytical function. By rereading and comparing entries over time, it becomes possible to identify trends, archetypes, and themes that reflect aspects of the unconscious. Dreams can contain symbolic messages, represent internal challenges, or even offer creative solutions to waking life problems. Over time, patterns emerge, revealing emotional and cognitive dynamics that can be consciously worked on. For those who wish to enhance their lucid dreaming skills, the systematic analysis of records allows for a greater understanding of their own dream triggers and the ideal conditions for lucidity to manifest. In this way, the dream journal becomes more than just a notebook: it transforms into a personal map of the dream universe, guiding the dreamer through a journey of self-knowledge and discovery.

Note-Taking Techniques:

Immediacy: Write down your dreams immediately upon waking, even if it's in the middle of the night. Dream memory is extremely fragile and fades quickly. Keep your journal (notebook, app, or recorder) always at hand, next to the bed.

Sensory Details: Don't limit yourself to describing the plot of the dream. Capture all the sensory details you can remember: Visual: Colors, shapes, objects, people, settings, lights, shadows. Auditory: Sounds, music, voices, noises. Tactile: Textures, temperatures, physical sensations. Olfactory: Smells, aromas, odors. Gustatory: Flavors, tastes.

Emotions: Emotions are a fundamental part of the dream experience. Note the emotions you felt during the dream, even if they seem disconnected or contradictory. Use precise words to describe your emotions (for example, instead of "happy," use "euphoric," "joyful," "serene").

Thoughts and Dialogues: Note the thoughts you had during the dream, the dialogues that occurred (even if they are fragmented or nonsensical), and any insight or idea that arose.

Title and Date: Give the dream a title that summarizes its essence or highlights an important element. Note the date and time you woke up.

Symbols and Metaphors: Pay attention to the symbols and metaphors that appear in your dreams. They may have personal or archetypal meanings (see Chapter 5 on the Psychology of Dreams). Write down your impressions and associations about these symbols.

Drawings and Diagrams: If you have difficulty describing something visually, make a drawing, a diagram, or a sketch. Don't worry about artistic quality; the goal is to capture the essence of the image.

Fragments: Even if you only remember fragments of the dream, write them down. Small details can trigger the memory of other elements of the dream.

Recurring Dreams: If you have dreams that repeat frequently, pay even more attention, as they may indicate important issues.

Analysis Techniques:

Regular Rereading: Reread your dream journal regularly, preferably weekly or monthly. This will help you identify patterns, recurring themes, significant symbols, and track your progress in the practice of lucid dreaming.

Pattern Identification: Look for patterns in your dreams: Recurring themes: What are the themes that appear most frequently in your dreams (for example, flying, falling, being chased, losing teeth)? Recurring characters: Are there characters that appear repeatedly in your dreams? Who are they? What do they represent to you? Predominant emotions: What are the emotions you feel most frequently in your dreams? Recurring settings: Are there places you visit repeatedly in your dreams?

Connections with Waking Life: Try to make connections between your dreams and your waking life. Do your dreams reflect your worries, desires, fears, internal conflicts, or recent experiences?

Symbol Interpretation: Research the meaning of symbols that appear in your dreams, both in symbol dictionaries and in Jungian psychology sources. Remember, however, that the meaning of symbols is highly personal and can vary from person to person.

Key Questions: Ask yourself questions about your dreams: What does this dream mean to me? What does this dream teach me about myself? How can I apply the insights from this dream to my life? Does this dream give me any clues about how to have lucid dreams?

Dream Signs: Identify the "dream signs" that are most common in your dreams. These signs are elements that indicate you are dreaming (for example, impossible things, people who have already died, bizarre situations). By familiarizing yourself with your dream signs, you will increase the likelihood of recognizing them during a dream and thus becoming lucid.

The dream journal, when used consistently and with the appropriate note-taking and analysis techniques, becomes a map of your inner world, a guide for the exploration of your unconscious, and a powerful ally on the journey to mastering lucid dreams.

Chapter 15
Adjusted Cycles

Human sleep follows a natural rhythm, regulated by the circadian cycle, which determines periods of wakefulness and rest over a 24-hour period. However, within this larger cycle, there are subdivisions called sleep cycles, each lasting about 90 to 120 minutes and composed of different phases. For those seeking to enhance their practice of lucid dreaming, understanding and adjusting these cycles becomes a powerful strategy. While direct induction techniques can be effective, manipulating the sleep pattern allows for the creation of favorable conditions for lucidity, increasing the time spent in REM sleep and improving dream recall. By aligning sleep schedules with the body's natural biology, it is possible to intensify the clarity and stability of dream experiences, facilitating the awakening of consciousness within the dream.

Each phase of sleep plays a specific role in the functioning of the brain and body. The initial stages of the cycle involve progressive relaxation and a slowing down of bodily functions, preparing the organism for deep rest. During slow-wave sleep, cellular regeneration and memory consolidation occur, which are fundamental for physical and mental health. However, it is in the REM phase that the most vivid dreams happen, characterized by intense brain activity and rapid eye movement. As the night progresses, periods of REM sleep become longer and more frequent, meaning that the last hours of nighttime rest are the most conducive to the occurrence of lucid dreams. Understanding this dynamic allows for the strategic adjustment of sleep schedules, maximizing exposure to REM and increasing the chances of achieving consciousness within dreams.

Adjusting the sleep cycle involves more than simply sleeping more or fewer hours; it's about synchronizing rest with the ideal phases for dream lucidity. Techniques such as Wake-Back-to-Bed (WBTB), which consists of waking up after a few hours of sleep and going back to sleep during the period of greater REM occurrence, can significantly enhance results. Other approaches include maintaining strict regularity in bedtime and wake-up time, taking strategic naps, and even experimenting with polyphasic sleep patterns, which fragment rest into multiple periods throughout the day. However, any adjustment to the sleep cycle should be done with caution, ensuring that the quality of rest is not compromised. The balance between discipline and listening to one's own body is essential to transform sleep cycle manipulation into an effective tool for the conscious exploration of the dream world.

As already mentioned in previous chapters, human sleep is composed of cycles of approximately 90 to 120 minutes, each going through different stages, including REM (Rapid Eye Movement) sleep, the phase in which the most vivid and memorable dreams occur. REM sleep periods tend to become longer and more frequent as the night progresses. Adjusting the sleep cycle seeks to take advantage of these longer REM sleep periods, increasing the probability of waking up during one of them or shortly after, facilitating dream recall and the induction of lucidity.

Understanding the Sleep Cycle:

Before adjusting your sleep cycle, it's important to understand how it works. A typical sleep cycle consists of:

Stage 1 (Light Sleep): Transition between wakefulness and sleep. Brain activity decreases, and it's easy to wake up.

Stage 2 (Light Sleep): Brain activity decreases further, body temperature drops, and heart rate slows down.

Stages 3 and 4 (Deep Sleep): Slow-wave sleep, essential for physical recovery and memory consolidation. It's difficult to wake up during these stages.

REM Sleep (Rapid Eye Movement): Brain activity resembles that of wakefulness, the eyes move rapidly under the eyelids, and the most vivid dreams occur. Muscle tone is low (sleep paralysis), which prevents the body from acting out dreams.

Sleep Cycle Adjustment Strategies:

There are different approaches to adjusting the sleep cycle with the aim of facilitating lucid dreams. Some of the most common include:

CAT Technique (Cycle Adjustment Technique): Already detailed in Chapter 9, this technique involves adjusting the bedtime and wake-up time on a specific day to interrupt a sleep cycle at a moment when REM sleep is more likely.

WBTB Technique (Wake-Back-to-Bed): Detailed in Chapter 10, this technique involves waking up after a few hours of sleep, staying awake for a short period, and then going back to sleep, increasing the likelihood of entering directly into a period of REM sleep.

Polyphasic Sleep (Advanced): Polyphasic sleep involves dividing sleep into several short periods throughout the day, instead of sleeping a single block of 7 to 8 hours. There are different polyphasic sleep patterns, some of which aim to maximize REM sleep time. This is an advanced approach and requires careful adaptation, as it can have side effects if not implemented correctly. It is not recommended to start polyphasic sleep without guidance.

Sleep Regularity: Maintaining a regular sleep schedule, going to bed and waking up at the same times every day, helps synchronize the biological clock and optimize REM sleep cycles. Sleep regularity alone can increase the likelihood of having lucid dreams.

Strategic Naps: A nap of 20 to a maximum of 90 minutes at strategic times can help; try it 6 or 7 hours after waking up and observe the results.

Important Considerations:

Individuality: The sleep cycle and the response to adjustment techniques vary from person to person. It is important to experiment with different approaches and adjust the times according to your needs and how your body reacts.

Sleep Health: Adjusting the sleep cycle should not compromise the overall quality of sleep. Make sure you are getting enough sleep and that your sleep is restorative. Chronic sleep deprivation can have negative effects on physical and mental health, as well as impairing the ability to have lucid dreams.

Combination with Other Techniques: Adjusting the sleep cycle is most effective when combined with other lucid dream induction techniques, such as MILD, WILD, reality checks, and dream journaling.

Patience and Persistence: Adjusting the sleep cycle requires time and practice. Don't be discouraged if you don't get immediate results. Continue experimenting and adjusting the technique until you find what works best for you.

By understanding and manipulating your sleep cycle, you will be creating a more favorable internal environment for the occurrence of lucid dreams, paving the way for the conscious exploration of your dream world.

Chapter 16
Persistent Dreams

Recurring dreams aren't just random mental replays; they're persistent messages from your unconscious, signaling that something needs your attention and understanding. They surface from the deep layers of your psyche, reflecting themes you haven't explored or internal conflicts that haven't been resolved. Unlike regular dreams that come and go without a pattern, recurring dreams insist on returning, often bringing the same settings, characters, or emotions with them. This repetition suggests an underlying meaning, a call for your conscious mind to wake up to latent and potentially transformative issues. When an image or story repeats over years, it becomes a powerful symbolic element, carrying an enigma that needs to be deciphered. These dreams are like echoes from your unconscious, reverberating until your conscious mind is ready to listen attentively.

Analytical psychology, developed by Carl Jung, suggests that recurring dreams are direct expressions of both the collective and personal unconscious. For Jung, they act as a mechanism for psychic compensation, bringing neglected aspects of your personality to the forefront or pointing to repressed content seeking integration. This recurrence can be linked to unresolved traumas, deep-seated fears, suppressed desires, or even transitional phases in your life. For instance, someone who frequently dreams of being chased might be dealing with a sense of threat in their waking life, even if they're not fully aware of it. Similarly, dreams of falling can symbolize a loss of control in some area of life, while dreams of dilapidated houses might reflect a need for emotional rebuilding. The key to understanding these dreams lies in carefully observing their details and being open to exploring their symbolic messages.

Working with recurring dreams not only deepens your self-understanding but also paves the way for significant personal transformations. The first step in deciphering them is recognizing their patterns and analyzing their core elements. Keeping a dream journal is a valuable tool, as it allows you to identify recurrences and draw connections between your dream experiences and your waking reality. Additionally, techniques like dream incubation, which involves intentionally focusing on a specific theme before sleep, can help direct your consciousness to interact more actively with these dreams. Another effective strategy is practicing lucid dreaming, where you become aware that you are dreaming while the dream is happening, allowing for conscious interaction with the elements of the recurring dream. By viewing these dreams as opportunities for self-knowledge, rather than mere sleep disturbances, you can transform their messages into tools for personal growth, making your unconscious an ally on your journey of individuation.

Psychology, particularly the Jungian approach, interprets recurring dreams as attempts by the unconscious to draw attention to unresolved issues, internal conflicts, traumas, fears, repressed desires, or aspects of your personality that need to be integrated. These dreams function as a psychic "alarm," signaling that something important is being overlooked or needs your attention.

Identifying Recurring Dreams:

Identifying recurring dreams is made easier by regularly keeping a dream journal. By rereading your entries over time, you'll start to notice repeating patterns and themes. Pay attention to:

Central Themes: What is the main subject of the dream? Is it about being pursued, falling, losing something, flying, taking exams, being publicly naked, finding treasure, or something else?

Characters: Who are the people who appear repeatedly in your dreams? Are they people you know, strangers, or archetypal figures (like the Wise Old Man, the Child, the Shadow)?

Settings: Does the dream take place in a specific location that you see again and again? Is it a familiar or unfamiliar place? What is that place like?

Emotions: What are the dominant feelings in the dream? Fear, anxiety, sadness, joy, anger, guilt?

Symbols: Are there any recurring symbols in your dreams? Objects, animals, colors, numbers?

Outcome: Does the dream usually end in the same way? Is there a pattern to how it concludes?

Using Recurring Dreams to Achieve Lucidity:

Recurring dreams can be a particularly good entry point into lucid dreaming. Because the dream's theme or setting is already familiar, you're more likely to recognize it while you're asleep. Here are some strategies for using recurring dreams to induce lucid dreams:

Pattern Recognition: Once you identify a recurring dream, become consciously aware of its pattern. Reflect on its theme, characters, settings, emotions, and symbols. The better you know your recurring dream, the easier it will be to recognize when it happens again.

Specific Reality Check: Develop a reality check specifically for your recurring dream. For example, if you often dream you're falling, make a habit of performing a reality check (like trying to breathe with your nose plugged or looking at your hands) whenever you feel that sensation of falling in a dream.

Pre-Sleep Intention (MILD): Before going to sleep, practice the MILD (Mnemonic Induction of Lucid Dreams) technique, focusing specifically on your recurring dream. Mentally repeat a phrase like, "The next time I dream I'm falling, I will realize I'm dreaming." Visualize yourself recognizing the recurring dream and becoming lucid.

Dream Incubation: Dream incubation is a technique where you intensely focus on a question or problem before sleep, hoping your dream will provide an answer or solution. You can use dream incubation to ask your unconscious to show you the meaning of your recurring dream or to help you become lucid within it.

Dream Rewriting: A powerful technique is to rewrite your recurring dream in your journal, but this time, change the ending. Imagine yourself becoming lucid in the dream and altering the course of events in a positive way. This helps to reprogram your mind and create a new response to the recurring dream.

Dream Dialogue: Once you become lucid within your recurring dream, you can not only change its course but also interact with the dream elements and ask why they are happening.

By actively engaging with your recurring dreams, you not only increase your chances of experiencing lucid dreams but also open a direct line of communication with your unconscious. This can lead to profound insights and personal transformations. The recurring dream, once a bothersome "alarm," can become a gateway to self-knowledge and the conscious exploration of your dream world.

Chapter 17
Rapid Induction

Inducing a lucid dream quickly requires techniques that leverage the delicate balance between wakefulness and sleep. The transition between these states is a strategic moment, in which the mind is not yet fully awake but retains enough consciousness to recognize and influence the dream experience. Among the various approaches to achieve this condition, methods involving subtle stimuli to the body and mind prove highly effective, as they allow the dreamer to slip directly into a lucid dream without interrupting the natural sleep cycle. Unlike techniques that rely on long periods of preparation or repetition of mental suggestions throughout the day, rapid approaches focus on the precise execution of small gestures or intentions at the right moment, favoring immediate results. Thus, exploring methods such as rapid lucidity induction represents an accessible path for those who wish to experience dream consciousness without lengthy training or complex meditative practices.

Among the most efficient techniques in this context, the FILD (Finger-Induced Lucid Dream) stands out, an approach that uses minimal finger movements to keep the mind alert while the body relaxes and falls asleep. This method benefits from the natural drowsiness that occurs upon waking up during the night or in the morning, when mental activity has not yet fully resumed its daytime rhythm. The key to success lies in the subtle interplay between focus and relaxation: the repetitive execution of a small movement prevents the mind from plunging into deep sleep unconsciously, while at the same time not generating excessive stimuli that could fully awaken the practitioner. This strategy is based on the principle that consciousness can be kept active through light mechanical actions, allowing the dreamer to enter the dream state directly while preserving their lucid perception. As a result, FILD enables a smooth transition to lucid dreaming, eliminating the need for long induction processes and facilitating entry into a universe of infinite possibilities.

The effectiveness of rapid induction also depends on adequate preparation and adaptation of the method to the individual characteristics of the practitioner. Some factors, such as the level of fatigue, the time at which the technique is applied, and the mental disposition to recognize the signs of the dream, directly influence the results. To enhance the effect of FILD and other similar approaches, it is recommended to combine them with habits that increase familiarity with dream states, such as practicing reality checks throughout the day and detailed recording of dreams in a journal. In addition, the conscious repetition of the intention to have a lucid dream before going to sleep can strengthen the connection between the waking mind and the dream world, making the recognition of the dream state more likely when it manifests. With patience and dedication, rapid induction can become a powerful tool for those seeking to explore the potential of dream lucidity, providing increasingly vivid and controlled experiences in the universe of dreams.

The technique is generally performed after waking up from sleep (either during the night or in the morning), taking advantage of a state where the mind is still drowsy and more receptive to suggestion. FILD can be used alone or in combination with the WBTB (Wake-Back-to-Bed) technique, enhancing its effects.

Step-by-step guide to the FILD technique:

Wake Up: Upon waking up from a dream (naturally or with the help of an alarm), avoid moving abruptly or opening your eyes completely. Stay as relaxed as possible, in the same position you woke up in. Ideally, you should be in a state of drowsiness, but conscious.

Finger Movement: Without making any other movement, begin to lightly move your index and middle fingers on one of your hands, as if you were playing the piano on a surface. The movement should be very subtle, almost imperceptible, requiring minimal physical effort. Imagine you are pressing the keys of a piano very lightly, alternating between the two fingers.

Focus on the Action: Focus all your attention on the finger movement. Feel the sensation of the movement, the light pressure of your fingers, the rhythm of the alternation. Avoid thinking about other things or letting yourself get carried away by daydreams.

Focusing on the action is crucial for the success of the technique.

Intention: While performing the finger movement, keep in mind the intention to become lucid. Mentally repeat a phrase like: "I am about to have a lucid dream," "I will realize I am dreaming," or simply "Lucid dream."

Reality Check: After about 20 to 30 seconds of performing the finger movement, stop and perform a reality check. The most common and effective test in this context is to try to breathe with your nose plugged. If you can breathe normally, even with your nose plugged, it is a clear sign that you are dreaming.

Lucidity: If the reality check indicates that you are dreaming, congratulations, you are lucid! Explore the dream environment, interact with the characters, fulfill your desires. If the reality check indicates that you are still awake, go back to performing the finger movement (step 2) and repeat the process.

Tips and Considerations:

Subtlety: The finger movement should be extremely subtle. There is no need to force or move your fingers excessively. The goal is to keep the mind minimally engaged, preventing it from falling asleep completely or waking up fully.

Patience: FILD may not work on the first try. Keep practicing, and over time, you will increase your chances of success.

Combination with WBTB: FILD is particularly effective when combined with the WBTB (Wake-Back-to-Bed) technique. By waking up after a few hours of sleep, staying awake for a short period, and then going back to sleep practicing FILD, you will maximize your chances of having a lucid dream.

Mental State: The ideal mental state for FILD is a relaxed, drowsy state. If you are too alert or too tired, the technique may not work.

Adaptation: Some people report success with FILD by adapting the finger movement. For example, instead of playing the piano, you can try lightly drumming your fingers on a surface, or simply imagine the finger movement without physically performing it.

FILD is a powerful and accessible technique that can quickly and efficiently open the doors to the world of lucid dreams. With practice and persistence, you can use this technique to induce lucidity on demand, exploring the unlimited potential of your dream mind.

Chapter 18
Conscious Awakening

Awakening within your own dream, becoming aware that you are dreaming, is a transformative experience that expands the boundaries of perceived reality. This moment of dream lucidity allows the dreamer to explore a malleable universe where the laws of physics can be bent and the deepest desires can be experienced without restriction. However, simply achieving this awareness is not enough to guarantee a prolonged experience. The excitement generated by recognizing the dream state can be so intense that, paradoxically, it leads to an abrupt awakening. The brain, detecting this excessive arousal, may interpret it as a signal to return to wakefulness, prematurely ending the dream. Thus, the true mastery of lucid dreaming lies not only in its induction but also in the ability to stabilize, prolong, and explore it with conscious control. To achieve this, it is essential to develop strategies that strengthen your presence within the dream environment, ensuring the experience unfolds fluidly and under your conscious direction.

One of the most effective ways to maintain lucidity within a dream is sensory anchoring, a process that involves actively engaging your senses to strengthen your immersion in the experience. When you focus on specific details of the dream scenario, such as the texture of objects, the sounds of the environment, or even the aromas and flavors present in the dream, your mind anchors itself in the experience, reducing the chances of a sudden awakening. This technique works because it reinforces the construction of the dream space, preventing it from dissipating due to a lack of conscious attention. Furthermore, subtle body movements within the dream, such as rubbing your hands together or slowly rotating on your own axis, help to reaffirm your presence within the dream state, creating a stable reference point for your consciousness. This type of interaction with the dream environment not only prolongs the experience but also strengthens your sense of control over the dream, allowing you to manipulate it more effectively.

Another fundamental aspect of sustaining dream lucidity is emotional regulation. Lucid dreaming can generate intense excitement, whether from the joy of realizing the freedom it provides or from the fascination with the richness of details and possibilities. However, if this excitement is not controlled, it can trigger an emotional surge that leads to awakening. Techniques such as deep breathing, repeating calming affirmations, and deliberately directing your attention to peaceful elements of the dream help maintain stability. Additionally, if lucidity begins to fade, methods such as fixing your gaze on a specific object, verbally reaffirming that you are dreaming, or even performing another reality check can restore the clarity of the experience. With practice and patience, it is possible to prolong lucid dreams and explore their vastness with greater depth, transforming each dream experience into a rich and revealing journey.

Therefore, just as important as learning to induce lucid dreams is learning to maintain lucidity after "awakening" within the dream. There are several techniques and strategies that can help stabilize a lucid dream, prolong its duration, and prevent premature awakening.

Sensory Anchoring:

As soon as you realize you are dreaming, the first thing to do is to "anchor" your consciousness in the dream environment. This means actively engaging your senses in the experience, paying attention to the sensory details of the dream:

Vision: Look around carefully. Observe the colors, shapes, objects, people, and scenery. Focus your gaze on a specific detail, such as the texture of a wall, the pattern of a fabric, or the face of a character.

Touch: Touch something in the dream. Feel the texture, temperature, and consistency of the object. It could be the grass under your feet, the bark of a tree, or the clothes you are wearing.

Hearing: Pay attention to the sounds of the dream. Listen to voices, music, and environmental noises.

Smell: Notice any scents in the dream. Is there a specific aroma in the air?

Taste: If there is food or drink in the dream, try it. Notice the flavor and texture.

This sensory anchoring helps to stabilize the lucid dream, deepening your immersion in the experience and strengthening your consciousness.

Body Rotation:

A simple yet effective technique for maintaining lucidity is to rotate your body within the dream. As soon as you realize you are dreaming, begin to slowly spin around your own axis, as if you were twirling. This movement, besides being enjoyable, helps to stabilize the dream and prevent awakening. It is believed that rotation stimulates the vestibular system (responsible for balance), which, in turn, strengthens consciousness during REM sleep.

Positive Affirmations:

Mentally repeat phrases that reinforce your lucidity and your intention to remain in the dream. For example: "I am dreaming and I will continue dreaming," "This dream is stable and long-lasting," "I have total control over this dream." Positive affirmations help to maintain focus and confidence, preventing doubt or fear from leading to awakening.

Interaction with the Environment:

Actively interact with the dream environment. Converse with the characters, explore the settings, manipulate objects, and perform actions. The more you engage with the dream, the more stable it will become.

Avoid Excessive Excitement:

While lucidity is exciting, it is important to control your excitement. Excessive euphoria can lead to premature awakening. Remain calm, take deep breaths, and focus on exploring the dream consciously and deliberately.

Return to Lucidity:

If you feel that you are losing lucidity, or that the dream is fading, try performing a reality check (such as looking at your hands or trying to breathe with your nose plugged). This can help to "reignite" your consciousness. Another technique is to refocus on a sensory detail of the dream, such as the texture of an object or the sound of a voice.

Maintaining lucidity in a dream is a skill that develops with practice. By combining these techniques and strategies, you will strengthen your ability to remain conscious within your dreams, prolonging the duration of the experience and making the most of the unlimited potential of the dream world.

Chapter 19
Astral Travel

The sensation of detaching from the physical body and exploring realities beyond the material world is one of the most intriguing and enigmatic experiences of human consciousness. Astral projection, often described as a separation of consciousness from the physical body, has been reported by countless cultures throughout history, always surrounded by mystery and fascination. Many who experience this phenomenon speak of the perception of floating above their own body, traveling through different dimensions, or accessing information that seems to transcend the common experience of dreams. Despite the lack of scientific proof, reports of astral projection have a remarkable consistency, suggesting that this experience may be linked to expanded states of perception. This out-of-body journey is often associated with spiritual practices, esoteric traditions, and even research into the nature of consciousness, being seen by some as a glimpse into a reality beyond the physical.

Although astral projection and lucid dreams are often discussed separately, there is a notable intersection between these two altered states of consciousness. Both involve a form of awakening within the subjective experience and can be induced by similar techniques. In lucid dreams, the dreamer becomes aware that they are dreaming and can actively interact with the dream environment, shaping it according to their will. In astral projection, there is a deeper perception of displacement, as if consciousness were operating outside the limits of the physical body. Some practitioners report transitioning from one state to the other spontaneously, suggesting that the boundary between these phenomena may be more fluid than imagined. The idea that astral projection is a specific type of lucid dream – more vivid and with a strong sensation of bodily separation – gains traction among those who study the experience from a psychological and neuroscientific perspective.

Regardless of the interpretation, the exploration of these altered states can bring significant benefits to self-knowledge and the expansion of the perception of reality. Many people who practice astral projection or lucid dreaming report an increase in intuition, a deeper understanding of themselves, and even a decrease in the fear of death, due to the feeling that consciousness can exist beyond the physical body. Techniques such as visualization before sleep, mindfulness practice, and the use of mental affirmations can help induce these states and deepen the experience. Whether viewed as a manifestation of the mind or as a true out-of-body journey, astral projection continues to arouse the curiosity and interest of those seeking to explore the limits of consciousness and access realities that go beyond the tangible.

There is a debate about the relationship between lucid dreams and astral projection. Some believe that the two phenomena are essentially the same thing, differing only in the subjective interpretation of the experience. Others argue that they are distinct phenomena, although they may occur in sequence or overlap.

Differences and Similarities:

Lucid Dreams: In a lucid dream, the person is aware that they are dreaming and can control the dream environment and their actions within it. The experience occurs within the dreamer's mind, in a world created by their own consciousness.

Astral Projection: In astral projection, the person has the sensation that their consciousness has separated from the physical body and is traveling in an environment that appears to be independent of their mind, whether it is the physical world (seen from a different perspective) or other planes of existence.

Connections:

The main connection between lucid dreams and astral projection is that both involve an altered state of consciousness, in which the person has access to experiences that transcend ordinary physical reality. Many techniques used to induce lucid dreams, such as WILD (Wake-Initiated Lucid Dream) and WBTB (Wake-Back-to-Bed), are also used to try to induce astral projection.

Some people report that, during a lucid dream, they had the sensation of separating from their body and entering a state of astral projection. Others report that, when trying to induce astral projection, they ended up in a lucid dream. This suggests that the two phenomena may be interconnected and that the boundary between them may be tenuous.

Theories:

There are several theories that attempt to explain the relationship between lucid dreams and astral projection:

Lucid Dream as Astral Projection: Some believe that all astral projection is, in fact, a particularly vivid and intense lucid dream, in which the person has a strong sensation of being out of their body. This sensation would be an illusion created by the mind, but the experience itself would be a lucid dream.

Astral Projection as a Type of Lucid Dream: Others argue that astral projection is a specific type of lucid dream, in which consciousness projects out of the body, but still within a dream environment. This projection would be a mental construct, but with distinct characteristics from common lucid dreams.

Distinct Phenomena: There are those who believe that lucid dreams and astral projection are completely distinct phenomena, with different mechanisms and natures. Astral projection would involve a real separation of consciousness from the physical body, while lucid dreaming would be a purely mental experience.

Continuum of Experiences: A more integrative theory suggests that lucid dreams and astral projection can be seen as part of a continuum of out-of-body experiences. At one extreme, we would have common dreams, without awareness. At the other extreme, we would have the "classic" astral projection, with the sensation of total separation from the body and exploration of other planes of existence. In the middle, we would have different degrees of lucidity and different types of out-of-body experiences, with overlapping characteristics.

Personal Exploration:

Regardless of the theories and debates, the most important thing is personal exploration. If you are interested in astral projection, you can use lucid dream induction techniques as a starting point. During a lucid dream, you can try to separate from your dream body, visualize yourself floating out of your body, or use other specific techniques to induce astral projection.

It is important to keep an open mind, record your experiences in a journal (whether of dreams or astral projections), and research the subject, seeking different perspectives and reports. Each person's experience is unique, and what works for one may not work for another. The most important thing is to explore your own potential and discover what works best for you. Remember that, whatever the nature of the experience, it can be a valuable source of self-knowledge and personal growth.

Chapter 20
Dream Stabilization

Maintaining lucidity within a dream is a challenge that demands a balance between control and immersion, presence and detachment. The excitement of realizing you are dreaming can be intense, leading to an abrupt awakening or a gradual loss of dream consciousness. To prevent the experience from being prematurely interrupted, it is essential to adopt techniques that stabilize the dream and prolong its duration. This process involves anchoring perception in the dream environment, emotional regulation, and the use of sensory stimuli to reinforce the connection between the mind and the dream. Just as a tightrope walker needs to constantly adjust their body to stay on the rope, the lucid dreamer must employ active strategies to sustain their presence within the dream state and fully enjoy this unique experience.

One of the most effective ways to strengthen dream stability is to intensify sensory involvement. Observing the details of the scenery, touching various surfaces, listening to the sounds around, and even experiencing tastes and aromas are ways to make the dream more vivid and prolonged. Touch, in particular, plays a fundamental role: rubbing your hands together, feeling the texture of objects, or walking barefoot through the dream environment are actions that reinforce your presence within the dream. Furthermore, focusing attention on small details, such as the patterns on a wall or the lines on the palm of your hand, helps to maintain the clarity of the experience. This type of sensory anchoring works because it keeps the mind engaged in the dream, reducing the tendency to oscillate between the dream state and waking. The more immersive the dream, the less likely it is to suddenly dissolve.

Another crucial aspect for stabilizing the experience is emotional regulation. Excessive enthusiasm can be as detrimental as doubt or the fear of waking up. To avoid this imbalance, it is important to maintain a calm and accepting attitude, remembering that the dream is a malleable space and that, even if it ends, new opportunities for lucidity will arise. Repeating positive affirmations within the dream, such as "This dream is stable" or "I am present and conscious," can reinforce your permanence in the dream state. Additionally, techniques such as slowly spinning around, shifting focus to a new scene, or even imagining a safe "escape point" within the dream can help to regain clarity when the experience begins to fade. With practice and experimentation, it is possible to develop a personal repertoire of strategies that ensure not only dream stabilization but also its deeper and more enriching exploration.

Dream stabilization is the set of techniques and strategies used to strengthen lucidity, deepen immersion in the dream, and prolong its duration. These techniques aim to anchor consciousness in the dream environment, reduce excessive excitement, and prevent loss of focus, allowing the dreamer to make the most of the experience.

Steps for Dream Stabilization:

Sensory Anchoring (Review):

As detailed in Chapter 17, sensory anchoring is the first and most important stabilization technique. As soon as you realize you are dreaming, involve your senses in the experience:

Look: Observe the details of the dream environment, fix your gaze on objects, colors, and shapes.

Touch: Touch objects, feel their texture, temperature, and consistency.

Listen: Pay attention to the sounds of the dream, voices, and music.

Smell: Notice the aromas of the dream, if any.

Taste: Try foods or drinks, if available.

This sensory immersion strengthens the connection with the dream and stabilizes lucidity.

Body Rotation (Review):

Also mentioned in Chapter 17, body rotation is another simple and effective technique. Slowly spin around your own axis within the dream. This movement stimulates the vestibular system and helps maintain lucidity.

Positive Affirmations (Review):

Mentally repeat phrases that reinforce your lucidity and your intention to stay in the dream. For example: "I am dreaming and I will continue dreaming," "This dream is stable and vivid," "I have total control over this dream."

Interaction with the Environment (Review):

Actively interact with the dream. Talk to the characters, explore the scenery, manipulate objects, perform actions. The more you engage with the dream, the more stable it will become.

Hand Rubbing: Vigorously rub your hands together within the dream. This simple action, in addition to involving touch, generates a sensation of warmth and energy that helps stabilize the dream.

Attention to Detail: Focus on a specific detail of the dream, such as the texture of a wall, the pattern of a fabric, the face of a character, or the lines of your hand. Observe this detail with full attention, examining every minute detail. This technique helps to deepen immersion in the dream and strengthen lucidity.

Remembering the Intention: Throughout the lucid dream, periodically remember your original intention. Why did you want to have a lucid dream? What did you want to do or experience? This reminder helps to maintain focus and avoid losing lucidity.

Avoid Closing Your Eyes: Avoid closing your eyes for long periods within the dream. This can lead to awakening or loss of lucidity. If you need to blink, do it quickly.

"Escape Point" Technique: When you feel the dream losing sharpness, imagine that there is a safe place, an "escape point." Use your intention and move there. This will recharge the stability of your dream.

Don't Worry About Waking Up: The fear and anxiety of losing lucidity often cause its loss. Accept that it is a dream, and even if you wake up, you can return to lucid dreaming.

Dream stabilization is a skill that develops with practice. Experiment with different techniques, combine them, and discover what works best for you. Over time, you will become more proficient at maintaining lucidity and prolonging your lucid dreams, paving the way for increasingly rich, profound, and transformative dream experiences.

Chapter 21
Controlling Emotions

The experience of a lucid dream provides an immersive setting where emotions emerge with singular intensity, becoming both a source of fascination and a challenge. Upon realizing that you are dreaming, the mind awakens to limitless possibilities: the freedom to fly, pass through walls, alter landscapes, or interact with dream figures. However, this very awareness can trigger emotional reactions that compromise the stability of the dream. The surprise of lucidity, the euphoria of control over the environment, and even the fear of the unknown can generate oscillations that destabilize the experience. The heart races, breathing changes, and the mind, when carried away by excitement or apprehension, can inadvertently cause an abrupt awakening or a gradual loss of lucidity. Thus, understanding and managing one's own emotions within the dream becomes essential to prolong and deepen this unique journey.

Emotional balance within a lucid dream is not about suppressing feelings, but about developing a conscious relationship with them. Intense emotions, whether positive or negative, carry enough energy to modify the dream state, often interfering with the continuity of the experience. If euphoria becomes excessive, the brain approaches the waking state, dissolving the immersion in the dream. If fear dominates, the experience can turn into a nightmare or result in an involuntary awakening. On the other hand, by learning to recognize and embrace these emotions without being swept away by them, the dreamer develops the ability to stabilize their presence in the dream world. Emotional control does not mean the elimination of spontaneity, but rather the creation of a point of equilibrium where excitement does not become an obstacle and fear does not limit exploration.

Building this control involves practices that engage both the mind and the body. Strategies such as conscious breathing, sensory anchoring, and the repetition of positive affirmations allow for modulating emotional intensity and maintaining clarity within the dream. Techniques of distancing and emotional transformation help to reframe feelings that could interrupt the experience, allowing the dreamer to remain present and conscious. With time and practice, this mastery strengthens, making it possible not only to prolong the lucid dream experience but also to use it more effectively, whether for self-knowledge, creative development, or simply to enjoy a universe where the only limitation is one's own imagination.

Intense emotions, whether positive or negative, can destabilize a lucid dream, leading to premature awakening or loss of consciousness. Excessive excitement, in particular, is frequently cited as a common cause of losing lucidity. This occurs because excitement increases brain activity, bringing it closer to the waking state and making it more difficult to maintain the dream state.

Therefore, learning to control emotions within a lucid dream is a crucial skill for anyone who wishes to prolong and deepen their dream experiences. It is not about suppressing emotions, but rather about managing them consciously, preventing them from dominating the experience and interrupting lucidity.

Strategies for Controlling Emotions:

Recognition and Acceptance: The first step in controlling emotions is to recognize and accept them. When you realize you are feeling an intense emotion (whether joy, excitement, fear, anger, sadness), do not try to repress or deny it. Simply acknowledge the emotion: "I am feeling joy," "I am feeling fear," "I am very excited." Accepting the emotion without judgment already helps to decrease its intensity.

Conscious Breathing: Conscious breathing is a powerful tool for regulating emotions. When you feel an intense emotion, focus on your breath. Inhale slowly and deeply through your nose, filling your abdomen with air, and exhale slowly through your mouth. Repeat this process a few times until you feel the emotion decrease in intensity. Conscious breathing helps to calm the nervous system and bring the mind back to the present moment.

Sensory Anchoring (Review): Sensory anchoring, already mentioned in previous chapters, is also useful for controlling emotions. By focusing on the sensory details of the dream (sight, touch, hearing, smell, taste), you divert attention from the emotion and strengthen your connection with the dream environment.

Positive Affirmations (Review): Mentally repeat phrases that reinforce your calm and control over the experience. For example: "I am calm and conscious," "I am in control of this dream," "I can feel joy without losing lucidity." Positive affirmations help to reprogram the mind and replace negative emotions with more positive and balanced ones.

Distancing: If the emotion is very intense, try to distance yourself from the situation that is causing it. Imagine you are an impartial observer, watching a movie. This emotional distancing can help reduce the intensity of the emotion and prevent it from dominating the experience.

Emotion Transformation: Instead of fighting against the emotion, try to transform it. If you are feeling fear, for example, try to transform the fear into curiosity or courage. If you are feeling anger, try to transform the anger into compassion or forgiveness. The ability to transform emotions is a powerful skill that can be developed with practice.

Humor: Use your sense of humor. Often, the simple act of laughing at a situation can dissolve a negative emotional charge.

Visualization: Mentally create an image that represents calm and control. It could be the image of a tranquil lake, an imposing mountain, a soft light, or anything else that conveys a feeling of peace and serenity to you. Visualize this image whenever you need to calm down.

Controlling emotions in a lucid dream is a skill that develops with practice. Do not expect immediate perfection. Start with simple techniques, such as conscious breathing and positive affirmations, and gradually experiment with other strategies. Over time, you will become more skilled at managing your emotions and maintaining lucidity, even in the face of intense dream experiences.

Chapter 22
Oneiric Self-Therapy

The human mind possesses a remarkable ability to heal and transform itself through subjective experience, and lucid dreams represent a privileged space for this process. Within the dream world, the dreamer can access deep aspects of their psyche, revisit memories, face emotional challenges, and reframe traumatic experiences without the limitations of physical reality. Oneiric self-therapy is based on the principle that by consciously interacting with symbols and emotions manifested in dreams, it is possible to promote profound emotional healing. The brain, by experiencing situations within the dream as if they were real, responds with perceptual and emotional changes that can have lasting therapeutic effects in waking life. Thus, lucid dreams become a powerful tool for those seeking to better understand themselves, overcome fears and blockages, and transform limiting patterns.

The therapeutic process within a lucid dream occurs through direct interaction with symbolic elements that represent emotional issues. Fears can manifest as threatening creatures, traumas can appear in the form of recurring scenarios, and personal challenges can be embodied by specific characters. Instead of avoiding these manifestations, the lucid dreamer has the opportunity to confront them safely, promoting the integration of repressed aspects of the psyche. This approach enables meaningful internal dialogues, changes in perception about past events, and even the development of new emotional responses. The plasticity of the dream allows the individual to recreate situations positively, replacing feelings of powerlessness with empowerment, fear with courage, and pain with acceptance.

Furthermore, the continuous practice of oneiric self-therapy strengthens emotional intelligence and psychological resilience. The simple act of setting the intention to resolve emotional issues through dreams already stimulates the mind to work towards healing. Upon waking, reflecting on the experiences lived in the dream allows for the consolidation of learning and its application in reality. Although oneiric self-therapy does not replace conventional treatments for severe disorders, it presents itself as a valuable complement, helping the individual access deep insights and build a path of self-knowledge and well-being. With persistence and sensitivity, lucid dreams can become a space for healing and growth, where the dreamer becomes the architect of their own emotional transformation.

It is important to emphasize that oneiric self-therapy does not replace conventional therapy with a qualified professional. If you are dealing with severe trauma or mental disorders, it is essential to seek help from a psychologist or psychiatrist. However, oneiric self-therapy can be a valuable complement to traditional treatment, accelerating the healing process and providing profound insights.

Step-by-Step Exercises:

Problem Identification:

Before starting oneiric self-therapy, it is important to clearly identify the problem you want to address. It could be a specific fear (of heights, animals, public speaking), a past trauma, a negative behavior pattern, a recurring feeling of sadness or anxiety, or any other emotional issue that is affecting your life.

Use your dream journal to identify patterns and recurring themes that may be related to the problem. Pay attention to dreams that evoke intense emotions, even if they are not lucid.

Dream Incubation:

Dream incubation is a technique that involves focusing intensely on a question or problem before going to sleep, hoping that the dream will bring an answer, an insight, or an opportunity for healing.

Before going to sleep, write down in your dream journal the problem you want to address. Be specific. For example: "I want to understand the origin of my fear of heights and overcome it in a lucid dream."

Visualize yourself facing and overcoming the problem in a lucid dream. Imagine yourself feeling calm, confident, and in control of the situation.

Mentally repeat a phrase that expresses your intention to have a lucid dream about the problem. For example: "Tonight, I will have a lucid dream about my fear of heights and I will overcome it."

Inducing Lucidity:

Use the lucid dream induction techniques you have already learned (MILD, WILD, WBTB, reality checks, etc.) to increase your chances of becoming conscious within the dream.

If you have a recurring dream related to the problem, use it as a trigger for lucidity (see Chapter 15).

Confrontation and Resolution (within the lucid dream):

As soon as you realize you are dreaming, stabilize the dream using sensory anchoring techniques, body rotation, and positive affirmations (see Chapters 17 and 18).

Summon the problem you want to address. This can be done simply by thinking about it, visualizing it, or calling it out verbally. For example, if you are afraid of spiders, you can say: "I want to face my fear of spiders now."

The problem can manifest in various ways: as a character, an object, a setting, a situation, or an emotion.

Confront the problem with courage and determination. Remember that you are in a dream and have control over the experience.

Use different strategies to deal with the problem, depending on its nature:

Dialogue: Talk to the character, object, or situation that represents the problem. Ask why it is there, what it represents, what it wants to teach you.

Transformation: Use your dream power to transform the problem into something positive or harmless. For example, you can turn a giant spider into a small, friendly spider, or a scary monster into a funny character.

Confrontation: Face the problem directly. If you are afraid of heights, you can imagine yourself climbing a mountain or flying without fear.

Reframing: Change your perspective on the problem. See it as a challenge, an opportunity for learning or growth.

Forgiveness: If the problem involves hurt, resentment, or guilt, practice forgiveness, both towards yourself and others.

Feel and express the emotions. Do not hold back or repress any emotions that arise.

Integration (after the dream):

Upon waking, write down all the details of the dream in your journal, including the emotions you felt, the strategies you used, and the results you obtained.

Reflect on the meaning of the dream and how it relates to your waking life.

Continue working on the problem in your waking life, using the insights and skills you developed in the lucid dream.

Oneiric self-therapy is a gradual and individual process. Do not expect miraculous results from a single dream. Be patient, persistent, and compassionate with yourself. With regular practice, lucid dreams can become a powerful tool for emotional healing and self-knowledge.

Chapter 23
Exploring Scenarios

The experience of a lucid dream allows for total immersion in alternative realities, where the dreamer takes on the role of creator of their own universe. Unlike the waking state, where the laws of physics and the limitations of the material world impose barriers, in a lucid dream the environment molds itself to the dreamer's will, making it possible not only to observe but also to interact with and transform scenarios with a simple thought or gesture. This power of manipulation is not restricted to the aesthetics of the dream but extends to the meaning and functionality of the dream spaces, allowing for the creation of environments that reflect emotions, desires, and deep aspects of the psyche. Thus, exploring scenarios in a lucid dream is not just an impressive visual experience but also a process of self-discovery, creativity, and personal growth.

The creation and modification of scenarios in lucid dreaming occur through intention and expectation. The mind, upon recognizing that it is dreaming, acquires a high degree of malleability, responding quickly to internal commands. Visualizing a desired environment with rich detail, fully believing in its materialization, and performing symbolic gestures to invoke change are fundamental strategies for shaping the dream world according to the dreamer's will. The continuous practice of this control stimulates creativity and strengthens self-confidence, allowing the individual to use dreams as a safe space for experimentation and expression. Furthermore, by exploring new scenarios and interacting with fantastic landscapes, the dreamer can access inspiration for artistic activities, solve problems from the waking world, or even overcome emotional blocks by creating environments that promote feelings of safety and well-being.

With time and practice, the ability to control scenarios in lucid dreaming becomes more refined, enabling instantaneous transformations and limitless expansions of the dream space. The dreamer can travel between fictional worlds, recreate places from the past, project futuristic environments, or even construct unprecedented landscapes that defy any concept of physical reality. This freedom provides a unique experience of exploration and learning, where every detail of the scenario can contain messages from the subconscious or serve as a stage for extraordinary adventures. More than a playful skill, the capacity to shape dreams becomes a valuable instrument for self-knowledge and for the expansion of mental horizons, allowing the dreamer to transcend the limits of imagination and explore the full creative potential of the human mind.

This ability to manipulate the dream environment is not only fun but can also be used for therapeutic, creative, and personal development purposes. You can use scenario control to:

Overcome fears and phobias: Create a safe and controlled environment to face your fears (for example, flying if you are afraid of heights, public speaking if you have stage fright).

Explore creativity: Create inspiring scenarios to compose music, write stories, paint pictures, or solve problems.

Practice skills: Simulate real-life situations to practice skills, such as speaking a new language, giving a presentation, or playing a musical instrument.

Fulfill desires: Experience things that would be impossible in the physical world, such as flying, breathing underwater, visiting other planets, or meeting people who have passed away.

Self-knowledge: Explore your own inner world by creating scenarios that represent your feelings, emotions, memories, or aspects of your personality.

How to Create and Modify Scenarios:

Clear Intention: The first step to controlling the dream environment is to have a clear intention of what you want to create or modify. The more specific your intention, the easier it will be to achieve. Instead of thinking "I want to be in a beautiful place," think "I want to be on a tropical beach, with white sand, crystal-clear water, and coconut trees."

Visualization: Visualize the scenario you want to create with as much detail as possible. Imagine the colors, shapes, sounds, smells, and textures. The more vivid your visualization, the easier it will be to materialize it in the dream.

Affirmation: Use verbal or mental affirmations to reinforce your intention. For example: "I am creating a tropical beach," "The sand is white and soft," "The water is crystal-clear and warm."

Action: Perform an action that symbolizes the creation or modification of the scenario. You can:

Point and Command: Point to an empty space and say, "A tropical beach will appear here."

Draw or Paint: Imagine you have a magic brush or pen and draw or paint the scenario in the air.

Build: Imagine you have the tools and materials needed to build the scenario.

Open a Door: Imagine that behind a door is the scenario you desire. Open the door and enter the new environment.

Spin: Spin around and visualize the new scenario materializing around you.

Snap Your Fingers: Snap your fingers and visualize the change happening instantly.

Expectation: Believe that your intention will be realized. Expectation is a crucial factor in lucid dream control. If you doubt your ability to create or modify the scenario, it will be more difficult to do so.

Persistence: If the scenario does not materialize immediately, do not give up. Continue visualizing, affirming, and performing actions until your intention is realized. Practice makes perfect.

Stabilization: Use stabilization techniques to keep your dream vivid.

Additional Tips:

Start with Small Modifications: If you are a beginner in lucid dream control, start with small modifications to the environment. For example, try changing the color of an object, making a flower appear, or altering the weather. As you gain confidence, you can try more complex creations.

Use Creativity: There are no limits to what you can create in a lucid dream. Use your imagination and creativity to create unique and personalized scenarios.

Have Fun: Controlling the dream environment is an incredibly fun and liberating experience. Take the opportunity to explore your creative potential and fulfill your most fantastic desires.

The ability to control the dream environment is one of the most powerful skills that lucid dreams offer. With practice and dedication, you can become the master of your own dream universe, creating and modifying scenarios at will, exploring your creativity, and expanding the limits of your imagination.

Chapter 24
Deep Journeys

Lucid dreams unlock doors to hidden dimensions of the mind, allowing for a profound journey into the subconscious. By becoming aware within the dream, the individual accesses a privileged mental state where memories, emotions, and unconscious patterns emerge symbolically, enabling an exploration free from the limitations of rational thought. Unlike waking reality, where mental processes follow a linear structure, in the dream world the mind manifests fluidly and creatively, connecting fragments of personal experience in unexpected and revealing ways. This immersion can provide insights ranging from understanding past traumas to discovering dormant talents, functioning as a powerful tool for self-knowledge and emotional transformation.

Delving into the subconscious through lucid dreams requires a structured and intentional approach. Before sleeping, setting a clear purpose for the experience increases the chances of accessing significant content. During the dream, techniques such as creating portals, invoking symbolic guides, and exploring metaphorical scenarios facilitate navigation through the deeper layers of the mind. Each element of the dream can contain a hidden message: a house can represent different aspects of personality, an ocean can symbolize repressed emotions, and a cave can indicate internal secrets waiting to be discovered. By consciously interacting with these symbols, the dreamer uncovers connections that would normally remain inaccessible in waking life.

Despite the enormous transformative potential of this practice, it is essential to approach it with respect and discernment. The subconscious can reveal challenging content, bringing to light fears and insecurities that were latent. Accepting these revelations without resistance, observing them with curiosity and without judgment, allows for the healthy integration of these parts of the psyche. Recording experiences upon waking, reflecting on the insights obtained, and seeking support when necessary, strengthens the process of assimilation and application of this knowledge in daily life. Over time, this conscious exploration of the subconscious not only deepens self-understanding but also strengthens the ability to manage emotions, make more aligned decisions, and live more authentically and balanced.

It is important to emphasize that the exploration of the subconscious in lucid dreams is not without risks. You may encounter disturbing content, fears, traumas, or aspects of your personality that you prefer to avoid. Therefore, it is crucial to approach this practice with caution, respect, and, if necessary, with the guidance of a mental health professional.

Techniques to Access Deeper Layers of the Subconscious:

Clear Intention: Before starting the "deep journey," define your intention. What do you want to explore in your subconscious? What questions do you want to answer? What aspects of your personality do you want to know better? The clearer your intention, the more focused your experience will be.

Dream Incubation (Review): Use the dream incubation technique (detailed in Chapter 20) to direct the content of your lucid dream. Before sleeping, focus intensely on your intention, visualize yourself exploring your subconscious, and repeat a phrase that expresses your goal.

Portals and Passageways: In a lucid dream, create a portal, a door, an elevator, a staircase, a tunnel, or any other passageway that symbolizes entering your subconscious. Visualize that, by crossing this passage, you will be accessing deeper layers of your mind.

Dream Guide: Invoke a dream guide, a character (real or imaginary) who can accompany and guide you in your exploration of the subconscious. This guide can be a mentor, a power animal, an angel, a deceased loved one, or any other figure that conveys trust and wisdom to you.

Dialogue with the Subconscious: Talk to the characters, objects, or scenarios that appear in your dream. Ask what they represent, what they want to show you, what message they have for you. Remember that, in a lucid dream, everything is a projection of your own mind, so dialogue with dream elements is, in fact, a dialogue with your own subconscious.

Exploration of Symbolic Scenarios: Create scenarios that symbolically represent your subconscious. For example:

A house: Each room in the house can represent an aspect of your personality or a phase of your life. Explore the rooms, observe the objects, open the drawers, look for hidden messages.

An ocean: Dive into the depths of the ocean, which can symbolize the deep unconscious. Observe the creatures that inhabit this ocean, the objects you find at the bottom of the sea.

A forest: Walk through a dense forest, which can represent the labyrinth of your mind. Observe the trees, the animals, the paths, the obstacles.

A cave: Enter a dark cave, which can symbolize the unknown. Explore the cave with courage, searching for hidden treasures (insights, memories, talents).

Meditation in the Dream: Find a quiet place within the dream and practice meditation. Meditation can help calm the mind, deepen lucidity, and facilitate access to unconscious content.

Automatic Writing in the Dream: Take a notebook and a pen (within the dream) and practice automatic writing. Let your hand write freely, without censorship or judgment. The words that appear may reveal messages from your subconscious.

Acceptance and Integration: When exploring the deeper layers, it is important to pay attention to emotions and accept them.

Important Considerations:

Self-Knowledge: The exploration of the subconscious in lucid dreams requires a good level of self-knowledge and emotional maturity. Be prepared to encounter challenging content.

Self-Care: Take care of yourself during and after the experience. If you feel overwhelmed or disturbed, stop the exploration and seek support.

Interpretation: Write down your dreams in your journal and reflect on the symbols, emotions, and messages that emerged. Dream interpretation can be a complex process, and the help of a therapist can be valuable.

The "deep journey" into the subconscious in lucid dreams is a journey of self-discovery that can bring transformative insights. With practice, courage, and respect, you will be able to unravel the mysteries of your own mind and use this knowledge to promote your personal growth and well-being.

Chapter 25
Dream Encounters

Lucid dreams offer an extraordinary dimension where the dreamer can consciously interact with dream characters representing different aspects of their psyche, memories, or universal archetypes. These interactions transcend mere entertainment, acting as bridges to self-knowledge, the resolution of internal conflicts, and even emotional healing. Within the dream environment, familiar or unfamiliar figures can emerge, laden with symbolism, reflecting hidden parts of the personality, repressed emotions, or valuable teachings. Whether conversing with a deceased loved one, seeking advice from a wise figure, or interacting with an admired fictional character, each encounter holds the possibility of profound and transformative discoveries.

The manifestation of these characters does not occur by chance. Clear intention and expectation play a crucial role in the materialization of desired figures within the dream. The subconscious mind responds to the dreamer's commands, so visualizing the character's presence, calling them verbally, or creating a conducive environment for the encounter significantly increases the chances of their appearance. Furthermore, understanding that each dream character, regardless of the form they take, represents a part of the dreamer themselves allows for more fruitful and revealing interactions. These encounters can bring unexpected answers to persistent doubts, offer new perspectives on real-life challenges, or provide intense and liberating emotional experiences.

For the experience to be enriching, it is essential to maintain lucidity and interact with respect and curiosity. Asking direct questions to the characters, observing their reactions, and paying attention to both their words and body language can reveal profound messages coming from the subconscious. Often, hostile or challenging characters represent fears, traumas, or repressed aspects that demand recognition and integration. Approaching them with empathy and understanding, rather than fleeing or confronting them aggressively, allows the dream to be transformed into a powerful tool for growth. With practice and openness to these interactions, dream encounters become a valuable channel for exploring the mind and personal evolution, making lucid dreams an even more significant and enriching experience.

These dream encounters can serve various purposes:

Self-Knowledge: Conversing with characters that represent parts of your own self (such as the inner child, the shadow, the ideal ego) can bring profound insights into your personality, your internal conflicts, and your potential for growth.

Conflict Resolution: Interacting with people with whom you have conflicts in real life (in a safe and controlled environment) can help you find new perspectives, express repressed emotions, and seek solutions to problems.

Advice and Guidance: Seeking advice from wise figures (real or imaginary) can bring inspiration, clarity, and direction in moments of doubt or difficulty.

Emotional Healing: Meeting with loved ones who have passed away can bring comfort, relief from longing, and the opportunity to say goodbye or resolve pending issues.

Creativity: Interacting with artists, writers, scientists, or inventors (real or imaginary) can stimulate your creativity, bring new ideas, and inspire your projects.

Entertainment: Simply talking with your favorite characters from movies, books, or games can be a fun and exciting experience.

How to Invoke Characters:

Clear Intention: Before attempting to invoke a character, clearly define who you want to meet and why. The more specific your intention, the easier it will be to realize the encounter.

Visualization: Visualize the character with as much detail as possible. Imagine their face, their voice, their clothes, their posture, their energy. The more vivid your visualization, the easier it will be to bring them into your dream.

Verbal Calling: Call the character by name, aloud or mentally. Say something like, "I want to meet [character's name] now," or "I summon [character's name] to this dream."

Creating a Portal: Imagine a portal, a door, a mirror, or any other passage that can lead to the encounter with the character. Visualize the character emerging through this passage.

Expectation: Believe that the character will appear. Expectation is a crucial factor in controlling lucid dreams. If you doubt your ability to invoke the character, it will be more difficult to do so.

Conducive Environment: Create an environment conducive to the encounter. If you want to meet a writer, you can create a library or an office. If you want to meet a warrior, you can create a battlefield or a castle.

Object Technique: Imagine that you have an object that belongs to that person, and concentrate on that object.

How to Interact Consciously:

Maintain Lucidity: Remember that you are dreaming and that you have control over the experience. Use lucid dream stabilization techniques (sensory anchoring, body rotation, positive affirmations) to maintain lucidity.

Be Respectful: Treat dream characters with respect, even if they are representations of negative aspects of your personality or people with whom you have conflicts. Remember that they are part of you.

Ask Questions: Ask the characters questions. Ask what they represent, what they want to teach you, what message they have for you. Be curious and open to the answers.

Listen Attentively: Listen attentively to what the characters have to say. Their answers can be surprising, revealing, and transformative.

Express your Emotions: Don't be afraid to express your emotions to dream characters. If you are feeling anger, sadness, fear, or joy, express these feelings authentically.

Observe Body Language: Pay attention to the body language of the characters. Their posture, gestures, and facial expressions can reveal important information about their emotional state and intentions.

Don't Get Carried Away: Maintain control of the situation. Don't get carried away by intense emotions or impulsive actions. Remember that you are the lucid dreamer and have the power to direct the experience.

Dream encounters can be profound and meaningful experiences that open a direct channel of communication with your subconscious and the world of symbols. With practice and intention, you can use this tool to promote your self-knowledge, emotional healing, and personal development.

Chapter 26
Dream Training

Dream training harnesses the vast potential of lucid dreams to refine skills with remarkable effectiveness. During the state of lucidity within a dream, the brain can simulate any desired experience with great realism, allowing the practitioner to hone their movements, reinforce mental patterns, and develop greater mastery over a specific activity. This technique is based on the principle that the brain doesn't fully distinguish between an experience lived in the real world and one vividly experienced in the mind. Thus, by training within a lucid dream, a person stimulates the same neural connections involved in physical practice, making learning and skill consolidation significantly more efficient.

Unlike simple conscious visualization during wakefulness, lucid dreams provide a dynamic and interactive environment, allowing the individual to feel textures, perceive sounds, adjust their performance in real-time, and experience authentic emotions associated with performing the task. This level of immersion increases retention capacity and facilitates the precise reproduction of the activity in the waking world.

The application of dream training can encompass various areas of knowledge and human performance. Athletes can refine their techniques by rehearsing movements with precision and controlled repetition. Musicians can perform complex passages of a composition, feeling the resistance of the strings, the instrument's response, and the flow of the melody without relying on physical practice. Professionals who need to handle public presentations, such as speakers and actors, can simulate various audience scenarios and develop greater confidence in their delivery. Even activities involving fine motor skills, like surgery or calligraphy, can be improved through conscious repetition in a lucid dream. Because the brain interprets these experiences realistically, ·nighttime practice reflects in daytime performance, optimizing learning without requiring physical exertion. Furthermore, dream training can be particularly beneficial for the rehabilitation of patients who need to recover movements or strengthen motor patterns after injuries, offering a means of practice without the risk of worsening their physical condition.

The effectiveness of this approach is supported by scientific studies that demonstrate the capacity of mental rehearsal to strengthen neural connections and improve performance in various fields. Upon waking, the brain registers the experiences lived in the dream as if they were real, allowing the new information to integrate into the individual's motor and cognitive repertoire. This technique also fosters the development of self-confidence, as it allows the practitioner to repeatedly experience the sensation of success, reducing anxiety associated with the actual execution of the task. Moreover, the lucid dream environment allows for testing innovative strategies, exploring new approaches to challenges, and even simulating specific difficulties to develop resilience in the face of unforeseen events. Thus, by using lucid dreams as a training ground, anyone can enhance their skills, overcome limitations, and accelerate their progress naturally and efficiently.

The advantage of performing mental rehearsal in a lucid dream is that the experience is much more vivid and realistic than simple visualization in a waking state. In a lucid dream, you can involve all your senses (sight, touch, hearing, smell, taste), experience the emotions associated with the activity, and interact with the environment dynamically. This makes mental rehearsal much more effective.

Scientific studies have shown that mental rehearsal can improve performance in various areas, such as sports, music, performing arts, public speaking, surgery, and physical rehabilitation. It is believed that mental rehearsal strengthens the neural connections associated with the practiced skill, preparing the brain and body for the actual execution of the activity.

Steps for Dream Training:

Define the Skill: Choose the skill you want to practice in your lucid dream. It can be anything from playing a musical instrument to giving a speech, passing an exam, practicing a sport, or performing a complex task.

Dream Incubation (Review): Use the dream incubation technique (detailed in Chapter 20) to direct the content of your dream. Before going to sleep, focus intensely on the skill you want to practice, visualize yourself performing the activity perfectly, and repeat a phrase that expresses your intention.

Inducing Lucidity: Use lucid dream induction techniques (MILD, WILD, WBTB, reality checks, etc.) to increase your chances of becoming aware within the dream.

Creating the Scenario (Review): Once you become lucid, create the ideal scenario for practicing your skill. If you want to practice a speech, create an auditorium with an audience. If you want to practice a sport, create a field, a court, or a track. Use the techniques for controlling the dream environment (detailed in Chapter 20) to make the scenario as realistic as possible.

Detailed Mental Rehearsal: Start practicing the chosen skill, paying attention to every detail:

Movements: Execute the movements with precision, feeling every muscle involved in the action. Sensations: Perceive the physical sensations associated with the activity (the touch of the ball, the weight of the instrument, the resistance of the air). Emotions: Experience the emotions you would feel when performing the activity in real life (confidence, concentration, determination, joy). Environment: Interact with the environment, observe the details, listen to the sounds. Result: Visualize yourself achieving the desired outcome (scoring a goal, playing the music perfectly, receiving applause). Repetition: Repeat the practice several times, striving for perfection in each repetition. If you make a mistake, correct it mentally and continue practicing. Variation: Vary the practice, simulating different conditions and challenges. For example, if you are practicing a sport, imagine yourself playing in different weather conditions, against different opponents, at different levels of difficulty. Record: Upon waking, note the details of your mental rehearsal in your dream journal. Describe the movements you performed, the sensations you experienced, the emotions you felt, the challenges you faced, and the results you obtained.

Benefits of Dream Training:

Improved Performance: Mental rehearsal in lucid dreams can improve performance in various areas by strengthening the neural connections associated with the practiced skill. Increased Confidence: Successful practice in a lucid dream increases confidence in your ability to perform the activity in real life. Reduced Anxiety: Mental rehearsal can help reduce anxiety associated with challenging situations, such as public speaking or competing in a sporting event. Overcoming Obstacles: Dream training can help you overcome mental blocks. Accelerated Learning: Practicing in lucid dreams can accelerate the learning of new skills, complementing practice in the physical world.

Dream training is a powerful tool for skill enhancement and personal development. By combining the vividness of lucid dreams with the effectiveness of mental rehearsal, you can accelerate your learning, increase your confidence, and achieve your goals more quickly and efficiently.

Chapter 27
Creative Insights

The human mind possesses an extraordinary capacity to connect ideas, generate innovative solutions, and bring abstract concepts to life. During lucid dreams, this creative ability reaches a new level, as the brain operates without the limitations of conventional logical thought, allowing unexpected ideas and unusual associations to flourish naturally. The dream environment, free from the constraints of physical reality, becomes a field of unrestricted experimentation, where forms, colors, sounds, and narratives intertwine to form valuable insights. By becoming conscious within the dream, the dreamer can intentionally direct this creativity, exploring scenarios, interacting with symbolic characters, and testing innovative hypotheses. In this way, lucid dreaming becomes a powerful tool for problem-solving, project development, and the discovery of new perspectives.

The creative potential of dreams has been widely recognized throughout history, with countless examples of artists, scientists, and inventors who found inspiration in their nocturnal experiences. However, unlike ordinary dreams, where ideas emerge passively and fragmented, lucid dreams offer a degree of control that allows the dreamer to consciously explore their own creative process. A writer can interact directly with characters from their story, observing their gestures and hearing their dialogues as if they were real. A musician can compose and play a new melody within the dream, experimenting with unprecedented sound combinations. A scientist can visualize abstract concepts in three-dimensional form, understanding new relationships between elements of their research. This type of experience not only facilitates creative production but also expands the horizons of thought, allowing the mind to go beyond what would be possible in a waking state.

Beyond direct exploration, lucid dreams are also fertile ground for the emergence of symbols and metaphors that can offer unexpected answers to creative challenges. Often, the solution to a problem does not present itself obviously but emerges disguised in seemingly random images, scenarios, and interactions. By recording and interpreting these elements upon waking, it is possible to discover profound meanings and new approaches to complex issues. Creativity, after all, is a process that involves both the generation of ideas and the ability to perceive connections between them. Lucid dreams enhance this dynamic, providing a space where imagination expands freely, allowing transformative insights to arise in surprising and innovative ways.

Many artists, writers, scientists, and inventors have reported finding inspiration in their dreams, both ordinary and lucid. History is full of examples of discoveries and creations that arose from dream experiences (see Chapter 3). However, lucid dreams offer an additional advantage: the possibility of actively interacting with the content of the dream, asking questions, experimenting with different solutions, and exploring alternative scenarios.

How to Use Lucid Dreams for Creative Problem Solving:

Define the Problem or Creative Challenge: Before going to sleep, clearly identify the problem you want to solve or the creative challenge you want to face. It could be something related to your work, your studies, your personal life, or any other area where you need a solution or inspiration.

Dream Incubation (Review): Use the dream incubation technique (detailed in Chapter 20) to direct the content of your dream. Before sleeping, focus intensely on the problem or challenge, visualize yourself finding a creative solution, and repeat a phrase that expresses your intention. For example: "Tonight, I will have a lucid dream that will show me the solution to [problem]" or "I will have a lucid dream that will give me inspiration for [creative project]".

Induction of Lucidity: Use lucid dream induction techniques (MILD, WILD, WBTB, reality tests, etc.) to increase your chances of becoming conscious within the dream.

Exploration of the Dream Environment: Once you become lucid, explore the dream environment in search of clues, symbols, metaphors, or ideas related to your problem or challenge. Observe the details, colors, shapes, sounds, smells, textures. Everything in the dream can have relevant meaning.

Dialogue with Dream Characters: Talk to the characters you encounter in the dream. Ask them about your problem or challenge. They may offer unexpected perspectives, wise advice, or creative solutions. You can even summon a specific character known for their creativity or wisdom (an artist, a scientist, a mentor, etc.).

Experimentation: Use your dream power to experiment with different solutions to the problem. Create alternative scenarios, test hypotheses, play with possibilities. Don't be afraid to make mistakes or try absurd things. The lucid dream is a laboratory of ideas where you can experiment freely without the limitations of the physical world.

Search for Symbols and Metaphors: Pay attention to the symbols and metaphors that appear in your dream. They may contain hidden messages from your subconscious, which may be the key to solving your problem or developing a creative idea.

Dream "Brainstorming": Provoke an "idea shower" in your dream, allowing your brain to present you with various alternatives, even if they seem disconnected.

Recording: Upon waking, write down all the details of your dream in your journal, including the ideas, insights, symbols, metaphors, solutions you experimented with, and the emotions you felt.

Reflection and Application: Reflect on the meaning of your dream and how it relates to your problem or challenge. Try to extract the relevant insights and apply them to your waking life.

Examples of Creative Use of Lucid Dreams:

A writer experiencing writer's block can use a lucid dream to visit the setting of their story, talk to their characters, and explore different plot outcomes.

A musician composing a new song can use a lucid dream to hear melodies, experiment with different arrangements, and find inspiration for the lyrics.

A scientist working on a new theory can use a lucid dream to visualize abstract concepts, test hypotheses, and seek new perspectives.

An inventor designing a new product can use a lucid dream to create prototypes, experiment with different materials, and test the product's functionality in a virtual environment.

Lucid dreams are a powerful tool for creative problem-solving and the development of new ideas. By combining the freedom of dream imagination with the consciousness and control of the lucid dreamer, you can access an unlimited reservoir of creativity and find innovative solutions to the challenges of your life.

Chapter 28
Facing Nightmares

Nightmares, though often terrifying, are powerful manifestations of the unconscious mind, bringing to the surface fears, anxieties, and internal conflicts that may remain hidden in waking life. Far from being merely disturbing experiences, they act as mirrors of the psyche, revealing aspects that need to be understood, processed, and, in many cases, transformed.

When a person experiences a nightmare, their mind is creating a highly symbolic scenario in which repressed emotions and traumas can materialize in the form of chases, menacing creatures, chaotic scenes, or helpless situations. These elements, far from being random, represent internal issues that may be being ignored or avoided in everyday life.

Therefore, learning to consciously deal with nightmares, especially within the context of lucid dreams, offers a unique opportunity for self-discovery and emotional healing.

Lucid dreams enable an active approach to resolving nightmares, allowing the dreamer to take control of the narrative and confront their fears directly. Instead of fleeing or waking up in panic, lucidity allows the person to question the elements of the dream, alter the course of events, and discover what lies behind the frightening experience. Many nightmares feature shadowy figures or threatening entities that, when faced with courage and curiosity, reveal themselves as internal aspects that need to be integrated into the dreamer's personality. A monster can symbolize an unresolved trauma, a chase can represent a responsibility that one is trying to avoid, and a claustrophobic environment can reflect feelings of oppression or lack of control in real life. By consciously interacting with these elements and seeking to understand them, it is possible to reconfigure the relationship with one's own fear, promoting emotional and psychological growth.

Beyond direct confrontation, transforming nightmares into positive or neutral experiences is a powerful technique to reduce their recurrence and emotional impact. With the practice of lucid dreaming, the dreamer can develop strategies to modify the nightmare scenario, alter the behavior of threatening figures, or even transform feelings of terror into sensations of calm and safety. A scary creature can be converted into a friendly guide, a hostile environment can become a welcoming space, and a dangerous situation can be rewritten to convey a message of overcoming. This capacity for dream manipulation not only strengthens the sense of control over one's own dreams but also reflects in waking life, providing greater resilience in the face of everyday emotional challenges. By learning to view nightmares as opportunities for understanding and growth, a person becomes more confident, balanced, and capable of dealing with their internal difficulties constructively.

Psychology, particularly the Jungian approach, interprets nightmares as messages from the unconscious, attempting to draw attention to unresolved issues, internal conflicts, repressed fears, or aspects of the personality that need to be integrated. By facing and understanding the meaning of nightmares, we can transform them into sources of self-knowledge and healing.

Lucid dreams offer a powerful tool for dealing with nightmares. By becoming conscious within a nightmare, you gain the ability to control the experience, to change the course of events, to confront your fears, and to transform the dream into something positive or, at least, less frightening.

How to Transform Nightmares into Positive Dreams:

Lucidity Recognition: The first step is to recognize that you are having a nightmare. This can be easier if you already have the habit of performing reality checks during the day and if you keep a dream journal, which increases your dream awareness.

Dream Stabilization (Review): As soon as you realize you are dreaming, stabilize the dream using sensory anchoring techniques, body rotation, and positive affirmations (detailed in previous chapters). This will help maintain lucidity and avoid premature awakening.

Fear Control: Fear is the predominant emotion in nightmares. It is important to control fear so as not to lose lucidity. Use conscious breathing, positive affirmations, and emotional distancing techniques (see Chapter 19) to calm yourself. Remember that you are in a dream and have the power to change the experience.

Confrontation: Face the source of your fear in the nightmare. It could be a monster, a pursuer, a threatening situation, or anything else that is causing distress. Approach the frightening element, look at it, talk to it.

Dialogue: Talk to the monster, the pursuer, or the threatening figure. Ask what it represents, what it wants, why it is there, what message it has for you. Often, the frightening figure is a symbolic representation of a fear, a trauma, or a repressed aspect of your personality.

Transformation: Use your dream power to transform the frightening element into something positive or harmless. You can turn a monster into a pet, a pursuer into a friend, a threatening situation into a safe one. Use your imagination and creativity to find the best way to transform the nightmare.

Reframing: Change your perspective on the nightmare. See it as a challenge, a learning opportunity, a message from your unconscious. Instead of feeling like a victim, feel like a hero who faces and overcomes their fears.

Creating a Positive Ending: Give the nightmare a positive ending. Imagine yourself overcoming the fear, resolving the conflict, achieving a goal, or finding a safe and happy place.

Integration: Upon waking, reflect on the meaning, as well as the emotions that arose.

Example:

You are having a recurring nightmare in which you are chased by a monster. Upon becoming lucid, you stabilize the dream, take a deep breath, and decide to face the monster. You approach it and ask, "Who are you? What do you want?" The monster replies, "I am your fear of failure." You then use your dream power to transform the monster into a small puppy. You pet the puppy and say, "I am not afraid of you. I accept my mistakes and learn from them." The nightmare turns into a pleasant dream where you play with the puppy in a sunny park.

By transforming nightmares into positive dreams, you not only alleviate the suffering caused by these dreams but also learn to deal with your fears and insecurities more effectively in your waking life. Regular practice of this technique can lead to greater self-confidence, emotional resilience, and psychological well-being.

Chapter 29
Emotional Healing

Human emotions, when not understood or processed, can create deep blocks that affect how a person lives, relates, and perceives themselves. Past traumas, unconscious fears, and negative thought patterns often subtly manifest in waking life, shaping behaviors and limiting personal growth. However, the subconscious holds not only emotional wounds but also the means to heal them. Lucid dreams offer privileged access to this inner universe, allowing individuals to directly connect with their repressed emotions, modify traumatic narratives, and experiment with new ways of dealing with their pain. Unlike the waking state, where the conscious mind often imposes barriers to introspection, lucid dreams create a malleable and safe environment for self-exploration. In this state, the dreamer can revisit past events, engage in dialogue with aspects of their own psyche, and transform their perception of difficult experiences.

The primary advantage of using lucid dreams for emotional healing lies in the possibility of actively recreating and reframing experiences. In a state of lucidity within a dream, the individual not only relives intense emotional memories but can also consciously interact with them, modifying elements, changing outcomes, and experimenting with different reactions. If a painful memory from the past still causes suffering, the dreamer can return to that moment within the lucid dream, but now as a stronger and more conscious version of themselves, capable of offering support to their inner child, confronting symbolic figures associated with the trauma, or even replacing a situation of fear and helplessness with a scenario of empowerment and resolution. This type of practice does not alter the facts of real life, but it allows the mind to process these memories in a less painful way, reducing their emotional charge and promoting healing from within.

Beyond working with past traumas, lucid dreams enable the integration of different aspects of the personality, especially those that have been repressed or denied throughout life. In analytical psychology, Carl Jung describes the "shadow" as the part of the unconscious where desires, impulses, and characteristics that the individual does not accept in themselves reside. In many cases, this shadow manifests in dreams through frightening or hostile figures, reflecting the person's internal fears and conflicts. However, instead of avoiding or fighting these elements, the lucid dreamer has the opportunity to confront and understand them. What once seemed like a threat can reveal itself to be an essential part of the personality that needs to be embraced and integrated. This process of acceptance allows for greater authenticity in waking life, reducing the need for social masks and promoting a deeper sense of emotional balance. Thus, by using lucid dreams as a tool for self-knowledge, a person can transform their relationship with their emotions, overcome internal barriers, and build a more solid and lasting state of well-being.

The advantage of using lucid dreams for emotional healing is that, within them, we can directly access our subconscious, where many of these issues are rooted. We can dialogue with the wounded parts of ourselves, express repressed emotions, rewrite traumatic narratives, and experiment with new ways of being and relating.

It is important to emphasize once again that emotional healing in lucid dreams does not replace conventional therapy. If you are dealing with severe trauma or mental disorders, it is crucial to seek the help of a mental health professional. However, the practice of dream lucidity can be a valuable complement to traditional treatment, accelerating the healing process and providing profound insights.

Practical Exercises for Emotional Healing:

Reunion with the Inner Child: Objective: Reconnect with your inner child, heal childhood emotional wounds, nurture your inner child, and reclaim joy, spontaneity, and creativity. Step-by-step: Dream Incubation: Before going to sleep, focus on the intention of meeting your inner child in a lucid dream. Visualize yourself embracing and comforting your inner child. Inducing Lucidity: Use lucid dreaming induction techniques. Creating the Scenario: Create a safe and welcoming setting for the meeting, such as a park, a garden, a beach, or your childhood home. Invoking the Inner Child: Call out to your inner child, visualize them appearing, and approach them with love and compassion. Dialogue and Healing: Talk to your inner child. Ask how they are feeling, what they need, what they are afraid of. Listen attentively, validate their emotions, offer love, support, and security. Embrace them, play with them, tell them you love them and that you are there to protect them. Integration: Upon waking, reflect on the experience and how you can integrate the needs and insights of your inner child into your waking life.

Dialogue with the Shadow: Objective: Recognize and integrate your shadow aspects (those aspects of your personality that you reject, repress, or fear), transform negative behavior patterns, and promote self-knowledge. Step-by-step: Dream Incubation: Before going to sleep, focus on the intention of meeting your shadow in a lucid dream. Inducing Lucidity: Use lucid dreaming induction techniques. Creating the Scenario: Create a setting that symbolically represents your unconscious, such as a dark cave, a dense forest, or a basement. Invoking the Shadow: Call out to your shadow. It may manifest as a monster, an animal, a frightening person, or any other figure that represents your fears, flaws, or repressed impulses. Dialogue and Integration: Talk to your shadow. Ask what it represents, why it is there, what it wants to teach you. Do not judge or reject it. Try to understand and accept it as part of you. Offer it compassion and love. You can even try to embrace it or merge with it, symbolizing the integration of the shadow. Integration: Reflect on how to integrate your shadow.

Conflict Resolution: Objective: Resolve interpersonal conflicts (with partners, family members, friends, colleagues) or internal conflicts (between different parts of yourself). Step-by-step: Dream Incubation: Before going to sleep, focus on the intention of resolving the conflict in a lucid dream. Visualize yourself dialoguing with the person (or the part of yourself) with whom you have the conflict. Inducing Lucidity: Use induction techniques. Creating the Scenario: Create a neutral and safe setting for the dialogue. Invoking the Person/Part: Call out to the person (or the part of yourself) with whom you have the conflict. Dialogue and Resolution: Talk to the person (or part of yourself) openly and honestly. Express your feelings, listen to the other's point of view, seek mutual understanding, and find a solution to the conflict. Integration: Reflect on the resolutions.

Rewriting Traumas: Objective: Reframe traumatic experiences from the past, reduce the negative emotional impact, and promote healing. Step-by-step: Incubation: Have the intention to revisit the situation in your dream. Inducing Lucidity: Use techniques to induce lucidity. Recreation: Recreate the scenario and the event, and change what is necessary to reframe the trauma. Integration: Upon waking, reflect on what the experience can teach you.

These are just a few examples of emotional healing exercises that can be performed in lucid dreams. With practice, creativity, and proper guidance (if necessary), you can use this powerful tool to transform your emotional life, overcome your challenges, and achieve greater well-being.

Chapter 30
Shared Dreaming

The possibility of sharing a dream with another person sparks curiosity and fascination, challenging the boundaries of the oneiric experience and human consciousness. Historical accounts suggest that, under certain circumstances, individuals can access a common dream environment, interact consciously within it, and upon waking, remember the same details with surprising accuracy. Although science has yet to find definitive evidence to prove this phenomenon, the number of testimonies and recurring patterns suggests that shared dreams may be more than mere coincidences. For those who explore the potential of lucid dreams, this possibility represents a vast field for experimentation, self-knowledge, and deepening the connection with other minds. If dreams can be shaped by intention, expectation, and training, then the construction of a shared dream space may be within reach of those who dedicate time and discipline to this practice.

The idea of a conscious encounter in the world of dreams is not new. Many spiritual traditions around the world describe practices in which shamans, monks, or entire groups accessed collective dream states to share visions, receive teachings, or perform rituals.

Furthermore, theories like Carl Jung's collective unconscious suggest that there is a deep layer of the human psyche where universal archetypes and symbols manifest, creating a common ground where minds can connect. Some recorded experiences indicate that people with strong emotional bonds, such as twins, romantic partners, or close friends, are more likely to report interconnected dreams. This suggests that empathy, mental attunement, and mutual intention may be decisive factors in the manifestation of this phenomenon. Even if shared dreams are not yet fully understood, their investigation opens avenues for reflections on the limits of consciousness, the nature of reality, and the unexplored potential of the human mind.

For those who wish to experience shared dreams, some approaches may increase their chances of success. Establishing a clear intention before sleep, visualizing a specific meeting point, and agreeing on a sign of recognition are strategies that can help guide the dream experience. Practices such as dream incubation, synchronization of sleep cycles, and the development of lucidity are fundamental to creating a mental environment conducive to meeting within the dream. Additionally, keeping a detailed dream journal and comparing notes with a partner can provide valuable clues about possible connections. Even if the results are not immediate, the attempt to explore shared dreams through conscious experimentation can strengthen dream awareness, deepen the bond between practitioners, and broaden the understanding of the mysteries of the mind and existence. Whether real in the physical sense or just a subjective construction of the unconscious, these experiences open doors to new forms of interaction and discovery within the vast territory of dreams.

The idea that dreams can be a space for encounter and interaction between minds is fascinating and has been explored in various cultures and spiritual traditions throughout history. In science fiction, shared dreams are also a recurring theme, portrayed in films like "Inception" and "The Abyss."

Exploration of the Phenomenon:

Despite the lack of scientific proof, reports of shared dreams present some common characteristics:

Planned Encounter: People who share a dream usually agree beforehand on the intention to meet in the dream world. They may set a time, a meeting place (real or imaginary), and a sign of recognition.

Conscious Interaction: Within the dream, people recognize each other, talk, interact, and in some cases, even collaborate to perform tasks or solve problems.

Subsequent Corroboration: Upon waking, people recount the experience, compare their memories, and discover that they shared significant elements of the dream, such as the setting, the characters, the events, and the emotions.

Sensation of Reality: Shared dreams are often described as very vivid and realistic experiences, with a strong sense of presence and interaction.

Theories:

There are several theories that attempt to explain the phenomenon of shared dreams:

Coincidence: Skeptics argue that shared dreams are just coincidences. People may have similar dreams due to shared life experiences, cultural influences, or simply by chance. Subsequent corroboration would be the result of suggestion, selective memory, and the tendency to find patterns where they do not exist.

Telepathy: Proponents of dream telepathy believe that minds can communicate directly during sleep, transmitting information, emotions, and images from one person to another. This telepathic communication would create the experience of a shared dream.

Collective Unconscious: Carl Jung's theory of the collective unconscious suggests that there is a deep layer of the psyche that is shared by all human beings, containing archetypes, symbols, and universal patterns. Shared dreams could be a manifestation of the collective unconscious, a meeting of minds at this deeper level.

Parallel Realities: Some more speculative theories suggest that, during sleep, consciousness may shift to other dimensions or parallel realities, where meeting other people would be possible.

Techniques for Shared Dreaming:

Although there is no guarantee of success, there are some techniques that may increase the likelihood of having a shared dream:

Partner Selection: Choose a partner with whom you have a strong emotional bond, trust, and affinity. The connection between people seems to be an important factor for the success of shared dreams.

Shared Intention: Talk about the intention to have a shared dream. Set a bedtime, a meeting place in the dream (a real or imaginary place), and a sign of recognition (a word, a gesture, an object).

Dream Incubation (Review): Before going to sleep, practice the dream incubation technique (detailed in Chapter 20), focusing on the intention to meet in the dream. Visualize yourselves meeting at the agreed location, interacting, and performing some activity together.

Lucid Dream Induction Techniques: Practice lucid dream induction techniques (MILD, WILD, WBTB, reality checks, etc.). Lucidity increases control over the dream experience and facilitates meeting the partner.

Record and Compare: Upon waking, immediately write down your dreams in your journals, without talking to each other. Then, compare your notes, looking for similarities, common elements, and signs that you may have shared the same dream.

Sleep Synchronization: Try to synchronize your sleep cycles, going to bed and waking up at the same times. This may increase the likelihood of you entering REM sleep at the same time.

Shared Reality: Talk frequently, establish agreements.

Technology: There are prototypes and models for sale on the market that promise to facilitate lucid and shared dreams.

It is important to emphasize that the practice of shared dreaming is experimental, and results may vary greatly. Do not be discouraged if you are not successful in the first attempts. Continue practicing, keeping an open mind, and recording your experiences. Even if you cannot prove the occurrence of a shared dream, the practice itself can strengthen the bond between you and your partner, increase your dream awareness, and provide fascinating experiences.

Chapter 31
Self-Transcendence

Self-transcendence is a phenomenon inherent to the human experience, characterized by the overcoming of ego boundaries and the pursuit of a broader connection with the universe. This journey of expanding consciousness has been explored by various cultures throughout history, utilizing rituals, spiritual practices, and meditative techniques to achieve altered states of perception. Among the most effective methods for this purpose, lucid dreams emerge as a powerful tool, allowing individuals to transcend everyday reality and enter symbolic and spiritual dimensions. Through the awakening of consciousness within the dream itself, it becomes possible to experience unity, ecstasy, and profound understanding, fostering transformative insights that resonate in waking life.

Mastering lucid dreams offers the possibility of exploring territories beyond the physical and psychological limits imposed by wakefulness. Within this expanded state of consciousness, the dreamer gains absolute freedom to interact with archetypes, access subconscious memories, and experience realities that defy the laws of logic and physics. Many accounts indicate that, by using lucid dreams for spiritual purposes, individuals encounter guides, masters, or symbols of wisdom who impart valuable teachings and guidance for their personal evolution. This experience not only strengthens intuition and the perception of reality but also provides a sense of belonging to the whole, dissolving the illusion of separation between the "self" and the universe.

To achieve self-transcendence through lucid dreams, it is essential to develop an intentional practice involving induction techniques, visualization, and surrender to the dream process. Establishing a purpose before falling asleep, whether it is the search for spiritual answers, meeting with beings of light, or immersion in states of ecstasy and illumination, directs the unconscious to create experiences aligned with these aspirations. Furthermore, the practice of meditation within the dream can enhance the depth of these experiences, leading to a direct connection with expanded states of consciousness. The integration of these experiences into waking life, through reflection and the application of acquired insights, transforms the dream journey into a powerful catalyst for spiritual growth and self-knowledge.

Lucid dreams, with their ability to expand consciousness and provide experiences that defy the laws of physics and logic, can also be used as a tool for self-transcendence and spiritual exploration. By becoming conscious within the dream, the dreamer gains the freedom to explore the dream world without the limitations of the physical body and limiting beliefs, paving the way for experiences that can have a profound impact on their worldview, values, and sense of purpose.

How to Use Lucid Dreams for Self-Transcendence:

Spiritual Intention: Before sleeping, set the intention to use the lucid dream for spiritual or transcendental purposes. You might ask to have an experience of unity with the universe, to encounter your spiritual guide, to receive a divine revelation, to explore other dimensions of reality, or any other objective aligned with your spiritual quest.

Dream Incubation (Review): Utilize the dream incubation technique (detailed in Chapter 20) to direct the content of your dream. Focus intensely on your intention, visualize yourself having the desired experience, and repeat a phrase that expresses your objective.

Inducing Lucidity: Employ lucid dream induction techniques (MILD, WILD, WBTB, reality tests, etc.) to increase your chances of becoming conscious within the dream.

Exploring the Infinite: Once you become lucid, explore the limitless possibilities of the dream world. Fly through the skies, pass through walls, dive into the depths of the ocean, travel to other planets, explore other dimensions. Let yourself be guided by your intuition and curiosity.

Encountering the Divine: Seek encounters with divine figures, beings of light, spiritual masters, angels, gods, or any other entity that represents the sacred to you. Converse with these figures, ask for guidance, receive teachings, feel the energy of love and wisdom that emanates from them.

Meditation in the Dream: Find a quiet place within the dream and practice meditation. Meditation in a lucid dream can be extremely powerful, leading to expanded states of consciousness, ecstasy, and union with the whole.

Creative Visualization: Use your dream power to create symbols and metaphors that represent your spiritual journey. Visualize yourself overcoming obstacles, achieving enlightenment, uniting with the universe, or any other image that resonates with you.

Surrender and Trust: Surrender to the experience, trust the wisdom of your unconscious, and allow the dream to guide you. Don't try to control everything. Let yourself be carried by the flow of the dream, open to surprises and revelations.

Integration: Upon waking, write down the details of your dream in your journal, including the emotions, insights, symbols, and messages you received. Reflect on the meaning of the experience and how you can integrate these learnings into your waking life.

Common Transcendental Experiences in Lucid Dreams:

Feeling of Unity: Losing the notion of ego boundaries and feeling one with the universe, with nature, with all things.

Ecstasy: Experiencing a state of intense joy, love, and bliss that transcends ordinary experience.

Light and Energy: Perceiving a white or golden light, feeling a powerful energy flowing through the body.

Encounters with Beings of Light: Conversing with angels, spiritual guides, ascended masters, or other luminous entities.

Journeys to Other Worlds: Exploring other dimensions, planets, parallel universes, or spiritual realms.

Revelations and Insights: Receiving messages, teachings, or revelations about the nature of reality, the purpose of life, or the spiritual path.

Death and Rebirth: Experiencing the symbolic death of the ego and rebirth into a new state of consciousness.

The practice of self-transcendence in lucid dreams is a profound and personal journey that can lead to significant transformations in the dreamer's life. By combining spiritual intention with the techniques of lucid dream induction and control, you can open a portal to experiences that expand your consciousness, deepen your connection with the divine, and bring you closer to your true nature.

Chapter 32
Dream Mastery

Absolute mastery of the dream world represents one of the greatest achievements on the lucid dreaming journey. When a dreamer reaches dream mastery, they transcend the limitations imposed by the unconscious and acquire an extraordinary level of control over their dreams. This ability allows them to shape the dream reality with the same ease with which they imagine a scene in their waking mind. The dreamer can manipulate environments, create complex characters, alter the laws of physics, and explore the boundaries of their own consciousness. More than just an exercise in control, this journey represents a profound immersion in self-knowledge and creativity, providing transformative experiences that challenge conventional notions of reality.

The path to this mastery is not immediate. Like any advanced skill, it requires continuous practice, experimentation, and a progressive refinement of perception within the dream state. Initially, the dreamer may experience difficulties maintaining dream stability or making intentional changes to the environment. However, as they develop greater familiarity with this space of limitless creation, they realize that their own belief in the possibility of control is the determining factor for success. Confidence and clarity of intention become the pillars of dream mastery. The stronger the conviction that it is possible to mold the dream according to their will, the easier it becomes to manipulate every aspect of this malleable reality.

Exploring the world of lucid dreams with full awareness not only expands the boundaries of human experience but also allows the dreamer to develop a deeper connection with their own subconscious. Through the deliberate creation of scenarios, characters, and events, it becomes possible to access hidden memories, confront symbolic fears, and even gain valuable insights into waking life issues. Interacting with dream elements takes on a new meaning when the dreamer realizes that everything within this universe responds to their mental and emotional state. This realization reinforces the idea that, just as in dreams, waking reality can also be influenced by beliefs, intentions, and perspectives. In this way, dream mastery is not limited to the sleep environment; it reverberates into everyday life, becoming a powerful tool for personal transformation.

Dream mastery is not a state that is achieved overnight. It is the result of years of practice, dedication, self-knowledge, and exploration of the dream world. However, there are advanced exercises that can accelerate the development of this skill and lead the dreamer to ever greater levels of control and awareness.

Advanced Exercises for Environment Manipulation:

Instant Creation: Instead of building the scene step by step (as suggested in Chapter 20), try to create the environment instantly with a simple thought or verbal command. For example, say, "Let a futuristic city appear now!" or simply think of the image of the city and visualize it materializing before you.

Large-Scale Transformation: Instead of modifying just one object or a small area of the dream, try to transform the entire scene at once. For example, turn a forest into a desert, a city into an ocean, a sunny day into a starry night.

Time Control: Manipulate time in the dream. Speed it up, slow it down, stop it, reverse it, or fast-forward it. Observe the changes in the environment and characters as you alter the temporal flow.

Gravity Control: Defy the laws of gravity. Fly freely, float, walk on walls or the ceiling, make objects levitate, create zones of zero gravity or inverted gravity.

Teleportation: Teleport instantly to other places within the dream. Think of a place (real or imaginary) and visualize yourself appearing there instantly.

Creation of Complex Objects: Create complex and detailed objects, such as machines, vehicles, works of art, musical instruments, technological devices. Explore these objects, manipulate them, use them to interact with the environment.

Character Creation: Create characters with detailed physical characteristics, personalities, and backstories. Talk to these characters, interact with them, observe how they behave.

Fusion with the Environment: Experience the sensation of merging with the dream environment. Imagine that you become the water of the ocean, the wind blowing through the trees, the sunlight, the earth beneath your feet. This technique can lead to experiences of unity and ego transcendence.

Manipulation of Your Own Form: Change the shape of your own dream body. Transform into an animal, a mythological being, an object, pure energy. Experiment with different shapes and sensations.

Dreams Within Dreams: Create dreams within dreams. Enter a new dream from your current lucid dream. Explore the different levels of dream reality. This technique can be challenging but can also lead to profound insights into the nature of consciousness and reality.

Breaking the Fourth Wall: Talk directly to the "dream" itself, as if it were a conscious entity. Ask questions, ask for advice, thank it for the experience.

Narrative Manipulation: Take on the role of the dream's narrator, controlling not only the environment and characters but also the story itself. Create plot twists, introduce new elements, change the genre of the dream (from adventure to romance, from comedy to horror).

Tips for Dream Mastery:

Regular Practice: Dream mastery requires regular and consistent practice. Dedicate time to lucid dreaming, practice induction techniques, explore the dream environment, experiment with different forms of control.

Confidence: Believe in your ability to control the dream. Confidence is a crucial factor for success. If you doubt yourself, it will be more difficult to realize your dream desires.

Clear Intention: Have a clear intention of what you want to do or experience in the dream. The more specific your intention, the easier it will be to achieve it.

Creativity: Use your imagination and creativity to explore the limitless possibilities of the dream world. Don't be afraid to try new and challenging things.

Self-Knowledge: The more you know yourself, the easier it will be to control your dreams. Explore your subconscious, your fears, your desires, your thought patterns.

Patience: Dream mastery is a gradual process. Don't be discouraged if you don't get immediate results. Keep practicing, learning, and exploring.

Dream mastery is a fascinating and transformative journey that can lead to incredible experiences and profound self-knowledge. By mastering the art of controlling your dreams, you will be opening a portal to a universe of limitless possibilities, where you are the creator of your own reality.

Chapter 33
Advanced Diaries

The practice of advanced dream journaling goes beyond simply noting down dream events, evolving into a profound process of self-discovery and exploration of the unconscious mind. A refined dream diary not only enables the identification of recurring patterns and enhances the ability to induce lucid dreams but also transforms into a powerful tool for understanding the symbolic messages conveyed by the subconscious. The richness of the recorded details broadens the perception of emotional states, manifested archetypes, and the connections between dreams and waking life, facilitating a consistent mapping of the dreamer's psychological and spiritual evolution.

Deepening the diary technique requires a conscious commitment to the precision of the record. Every sensory detail of the dream – colors, textures, sounds, temperatures, and even tactile sensations – must be described with the utmost accuracy. This wealth of information allows for a clearer reconstruction of the dream upon rereading, making it easier to analyze its nuances and identify triggers that can aid in inducing future lucid dreams. Furthermore, the inclusion of detailed emotional aspects enables a more comprehensive understanding of the internal reactions to the dream content, revealing profound aspects of the psyche that often go unnoticed in waking life.

More than just a repository of nighttime experiences, an advanced dream diary can become a true experimental laboratory for testing induction techniques, dream manipulation, and exploration of the unconscious. By regularly reviewing the entries, hidden patterns emerge, allowing the dreamer to better understand the central themes that permeate their psychic life. The comparative study of dreams over time can reveal the progression of an internal process of transformation, yielding valuable insights into personal challenges, spiritual growth, and the interplay between the inner and outer worlds. In this way, the diary transforms into a portal for self-transcendence, fostering not only greater control over dreams but also a profound impact on waking life.

Advanced Recording Techniques:

Detailed Multisensory Recording: Beyond describing the dream's plot, meticulously record all sensory details, even those that seem insignificant:

Visual: Colors (specific shades, brightness, contrast), shapes (geometric, organic, abstract), textures (smooth, rough, soft, coarse), light and shadow (intensity, direction, light sources), movement (speed, direction, rhythm).

Auditory: Sounds (volume, tone, timbre), music (melody, rhythm, instruments), voices (tone, accent, emotion), noises (nature, machines, crowds).

Tactile: Textures (hot, cold, humid, dry), pressure, weight, pain, pleasure.

Olfactory: Smells (pleasant, unpleasant, familiar, unknown), aromas (flowers, food, perfumes).

Gustatory: Flavors (sweet, salty, bitter, sour, spicy), textures (creamy, crunchy, liquid).

Kinesthetic: Sensations of movement (flying, falling, spinning, running), balance, proprioception (perception of the body's position in space).

Deep Emotional Recording: Explore the emotions felt during the dream in depth. Don't limit yourself to generic labels like "happy," "sad," or "scared." Use more precise and descriptive words:

Instead of "happy," use "euphoric," "joyful," "serene," "grateful," "ecstatic."

Instead of "sad," use "melancholic," "hopeless," "anguished," "helpless."

Instead of "scared," use "terrified," "anxious," "apprehensive," "restless."

Also, note the variations in the intensity of emotions throughout the dream. An emotion might start weak and intensify, or vice versa.

Recording Thoughts and Dialogues: Write down all the thoughts you had during the dream, even if they seem irrelevant or disconnected. Also, record dialogues as completely as possible, including the tone of voice, body language, and emotions of the speakers.

Detailed Drawings and Diagrams: Use drawings, diagrams, maps, graphs, or any other visual aid to complement the written record. Don't worry about artistic quality; the goal is to capture the essence of the dream experience.

Symbols and Metaphors (Immediate Interpretation): Next to the dream entry, immediately jot down your impressions and associations about the symbols and metaphors that appeared. What is the personal meaning of these symbols for you? What do they represent in your life? This immediate interpretation, made before the rational mind takes over, can be very revealing.

Audio Recording: If you find it difficult to write upon waking, use an audio recorder to record your dreams. The recording can capture nuances in your voice, such as emotion and hesitation, which might be lost in a written account.

Advanced Analysis Techniques:

Longitudinal Analysis: Analyze your dream diary from a long-term perspective, looking for patterns, themes, and symbols that repeat over months or years. This analysis can reveal deep issues from your unconscious that are being processed at a more subtle level.

Comparative Analysis: Compare your dreams with the dreams of other people (lucid dream partners, friends, family, or accounts in books and articles). This comparison can provide insights into the nature of dreams and your own dream experience.

Archetypal Analysis (Jung): Utilize the concepts of Jungian psychology (archetypes, shadow, anima/animus, collective unconscious) to interpret your dreams. Look for universal symbols and patterns of behavior that manifest in your dreams.

Content Analysis: Use content analysis techniques to identify the frequency of words, themes, emotions, and characters in your dreams. This quantitative analysis can complement the qualitative analysis and reveal patterns that might go unnoticed. Use computer tools to perform this analysis.

Correlation with Life Events: Try to correlate the themes and emotions of your dreams with events in your waking life. Do your dreams reflect your worries, desires, fears, or conflicts? Is there a relationship between your dreams and your relationships, work, health, or spirituality?

Dream Experimentation: Use your dream diary as a laboratory for experimentation. Note the induction techniques you use, the results you obtain, and the experiments you conduct in your lucid dreams (such as trying to fly, change scenery, or talk to dream characters).

Lucid Dream Planning: Use your diary to plan your next lucid dreams. Set intentions, visualize scenarios, and prepare questions to ask dream characters.

The advanced dream diary becomes a mirror of your soul, a map of your unconscious, and a guide for your journey of self-discovery. By deepening your use of this tool, you will be opening a direct channel of communication with the deepest and wisest part of yourself, accessing insights that can transform your life.

Chapter 34
Beyond Dreaming

The journey of lucid dreaming doesn't end upon waking; rather, it continues to unfold in waking life, influencing perception, behavior, and how one interacts with the world. The experiences lived in the dream world carry profound insights into the psyche, reveal hidden aspects of personality, and offer opportunities for learning and transformation. Integrating this knowledge into everyday life means opening a direct channel between the conscious and unconscious mind, allowing what was discovered in the dream to manifest in reality in a tangible and meaningful way. This process of integration not only broadens self-understanding but also enhances personal development in various areas, such as creativity, emotional intelligence, and problem-solving.

The practical application of lessons drawn from lucid dreams can take different forms. Self-analysis, based on reflection on dream events, allows for the identification of emotional and psychological patterns that repeat both in dreams and in waking life. Through this process, it becomes possible to better understand fears, desires, limitations, and unexplored potentials. Furthermore, the practice of consciously visualizing the scenarios and emotions experienced in the dream can serve as a tool to reinforce positive feelings and facilitate the change of limiting behaviors. By recalling and mentally reliving the sensations of empowerment, freedom, and creativity experienced in a lucid dream, the dreamer strengthens their ability to bring these qualities into wakefulness, transforming their approach to daily challenges.

Another fundamental aspect of integrating lucid dreams into daily life is the application of skills developed in the dream state. Techniques such as mental rehearsal, where the dreamer practices a certain activity within the dream to improve it in waking life, can be extremely effective in enhancing physical and cognitive performance. Moreover, the flexibility of the mind during lucid dreams stimulates creativity and innovation, allowing new ideas and original solutions to emerge more easily in the waking state. When one understands that the dream world is not an isolated space but rather a fertile ground for growth and self-discovery, the experience of dreaming becomes a valuable resource for enriching life in a profound and transformative way.

Integrating Dream Insights:

Reflection and Self-Analysis:

Take time to reflect on your lucid dreams and the messages they bring. Use your dream journal as a guide, revisit notes, drawings, and interpretations. Ask yourself:

What did this dream teach me about myself?

What aspects of my personality were revealed or explored in the dream?

What emotions were awakened or processed in the dream?

What challenges were faced or overcome in the dream?

What insights or creative solutions arose in the dream?

How can I apply these learnings to my waking life?

Conscious Action: Turn dream insights into concrete actions in your waking life. If you overcame a fear in a lucid dream, try to face that fear in reality, step by step. If you received advice from a dream guide, try to put it into practice. If you discovered a new talent or skill in the dream, explore that area in your waking life.

Behavior Change: Use lucid dreams as a laboratory to experiment with new ways of being and relating. If you practiced assertiveness in a dream, try to be more assertive in your daily interactions. If you experienced compassion in a dream, try to cultivate that quality in your waking life.

Problem Solving: Apply the creative solutions you found in your lucid dreams to the problems in your real life. If you visualized a new approach to a work project, try to implement it. If you dreamed of a way to resolve a conflict with a friend, try talking to them using that new perspective.

Creative Expression: Use lucid dreams as a source of inspiration for your creative expression. If you dreamed of a song, try to compose it. If you dreamed of a painting, try to paint it. If you dreamed of a story, try to write it.

Integrating Dream Emotions:

Validation of Emotions: Recognize and validate the emotions you felt in your lucid dreams, even if they seem intense or uncomfortable. Dream emotions are real and can provide important clues about your emotional state.

Emotional Processing: If you experienced difficult emotions in a lucid dream (fear, sadness, anger, guilt), set aside time to process them in your waking life. Talk to a friend, a therapist, write in your journal, practice meditation, or use any other technique that helps you deal with these emotions in a healthy way.

Cultivating Positive Emotions: If you experienced positive emotions in a lucid dream (joy, love, gratitude, confidence), try to cultivate these emotions in your waking life. Remember the feeling of the dream, visualize yourself feeling those emotions again, and look for opportunities to express them in your daily interactions.

Integrating Dream Skills:

Mental Rehearsal: Use the technique of mental rehearsal (practiced in lucid dreams) to improve your skills in your waking life. Visualize yourself performing the activity perfectly, feeling the same emotions and sensations you experienced in the dream.

Mindfulness: The practice of mindfulness, cultivated in meditation and reality checks, can be applied in your daily life. Be present in the moment, observe your thoughts and emotions without judgment, pay attention to the details of your surroundings.

Emotional Control: The emotional control techniques learned in lucid dreams (conscious breathing, positive affirmations, detachment) can be used in challenging real-life situations.

Creativity: The freedom and flexibility experienced in lucid dreams can inspire your creativity in your waking life. Allow yourself to think outside the box, experiment with new ideas, and seek innovative solutions.

The integration of dream experiences into waking life is a continuous and gradual process. Don't expect radical changes overnight. Be patient with yourself, celebrate every small progress, and continue exploring the transformative potential of your dreams. By building this bridge between the dream world and everyday reality, you will be enriching your life, expanding your consciousness, and walking a path of self-knowledge and personal growth.

Epilogue

And now that you have reached the end of this journey, ask yourself: what has changed?

From the moment you began reading, you were led through a universe invisible to the naked eye, yet as real as any other experience you have ever lived. Each chapter revealed secrets about the dream world, offering techniques, reflections, and knowledge capable of transforming not only your dreams but also your perception of waking reality.

But the true learning doesn't end here. Quite the contrary: this is just the beginning.

You may have learned to identify when you are dreaming. You may have understood how reality checks work. You may have even already experienced lucid dreaming, feeling the indescribable excitement of realizing you are inside a dream and taking control of it. But there is something even deeper and more transformative in this process: the discovery that dreams reflect who you are.

Each lucid dream is a mirror of your mind, revealing not only your desires but also your fears, your uncertainties, and your purest essence. By mastering this art, you not only control nighttime narratives – you become an explorer of your own unconscious. Dreams become a laboratory for creativity, a training ground for your courage, and a bridge to self-knowledge.

And then, a new question arises: if you can awaken within your dreams, why not awaken within life itself?

The reality you live now is, in many ways, a dream shaped by your perceptions and beliefs. Just like in the dream world, there are rules that seem immutable – but which, when questioned, prove to be more flexible than you imagine. Just like in a lucid dream, you have the power to transform scenarios, challenge expectations, and create your own narrative. The only difference is that, unlike sleep, wakefulness doesn't end when you open your eyes.

Awakening to lucidity in dreams is just a prelude to an even greater awakening: awakening to conscious living.

May this book not only be a source of technical knowledge but an invitation to the most fascinating exploration that exists – the journey into yourself. For those who master the art of controlling dreams don't just sleep better... they live better.

And now, the final question: what will you do with this knowledge?

The answer, just like your dreams, is in your hands.